Each for the Other

Also by Bryan Chapell

Christ-Centered Preaching
In the Grip of Grace
Standing Your Ground
Using Illustrations to Preach with Power

Each for the Other

Marriage As It's Meant to Be

Bryan Chapell

Baker Books

A Division of Baker Book House Co
Grand Rapids, Michigan 49516

Published by Baker Books
a division of Baker Book House Company
P.O. Box 6287, Grand Rapids, MI 49516-6287

Printed in the United States of America

Library of Congress Cataloging-in-Publication Data

Chapell, Bryan.
    Each for the other : marriage as it's meant to be / Bryan Chapell.
      c. cm.
    ISBN 0-8010-1181-7
    1. Spouses—Religious life. 2. Marriage—religious aspect—Christianity.
I. Title.
BV4596.M3C48   1999
248.8'44—dc21   98-42906

A small-group leader's guide for *Each for the Other* may be ordered through the Media Office of Covenant Theological Seminary, 12330 Conway Road, St. Louis, MO 63141, 314-434-4044.

Names of individuals and occasional specifics are changed in some personal accounts appearing in this book to respect the concerns and wishes of those involved. My debt is great to those who have taught me the realities of Christ's love by the testimony of their lives.

For current information about all releases from Baker Book House, visit our web site:
http://www.bakerbooks.com

To Kathy, my wife, whose love yields
joy,
strength,
comfort,
courage,
and
faith.

In loving her, I find more of
myself,
more ability to love,
and
more of the love of my Savior.

Through her love, our children,
Colin,
Jordan,
Corinne,
and
Kaitlin,
bring us joy, pride, humility, and more faith.

In my absences, Kathy has been our family's heart.
In my busyness, she has been our family's care.
In my awkwardness, she has been our tenderness.
We rise up and call her God's great blessing
on our home (Prov. 31:28).

Contents

Who's in Charge?

They knew their marriage was coming apart when they came to see me. Though each claimed to be trying to "live what the Bible says," love had drained from their relationship. The reason was not obvious. Both had come from families that frequented church and both were well schooled in the Bible. They had even met at a Christian college. I detected nothing in their background that could account for the tensions the couple was now experiencing.

I asked the young man for his explanation of their troubled marriage. He expressed genuine consternation. He said that he had tried be a good husband. Because his college had strongly emphasized the importance of following biblical family models, he had committed himself to being a spiritual leader in his home. I asked him to explain in everyday terms how he expressed his leadership. This is what he said:

"In order to make sure there is no question about who is the head of our home, I try to make sure both my wife and I let Scripture rule our actions. For instance, even when I come home from work and want to relax, I still try to act as the head of my home. If my wife asks for some help with something in the kitchen, or with the kids [he had three preschoolers, including a set of twins], I don't immediately drop my newspaper and snap to attention. To make sure we both understand who is the head of our home, I flip a coin in my mind. If it comes up heads, I help. If it comes up tails, I don't. That way there's no question of who's in charge."

Now I thought I was beginning to get an idea of where some of the problems in this marriage might lie. But why? Though this man's actions may seem extreme, the Bible does say that the husband is the "head" of the home and that the wife should "submit" to him. Scripture gives a husband a right—even a responsibility—to keep spousal roles clear. If we are unwilling to throw away scriptural passages that require the exercise of authority, then how do we know that such conduct in marriage is wrong?

Finding biblical answers to this question will require us to go beyond a surface reading of Scripture that would seem to justify dictatorial rule by one spouse or to require the abandonment of personal dignity by another. We will discover that such readings do not submit to the deeper truths of God's Word concerning loving relationships in Christian homes.

The Glories of Sacrifice

Access to the deeper dimensions of the Bible's instruction requires no secret codes, special revelations, or privileged insights. Minds and hearts open to the core message of Scripture recognize that God neither commends nor commands selfishness. When the ruler of the universe in the person of Jesus Christ gave his life on a cross to rescue us from the consequences of our own sin, he taught us the glory of sacrifice. Jesus said, "Whoever finds his life will lose it, and whoever loses his life for my sake will find it" (Matt. 10:39). Lives devoted merely to serving self cannot avoid making one's own desires the goal and god of every action. Such whimsical gods ultimately enslave people to their own appetites.

God designed us to know life's greatest fulfillment through losing ourselves in the service of purposes higher than self-satisfaction. When a marriage is built on the premise that one person may find happiness by using another, the deepest passions God has placed in hearts in which his Spirit lives are ignored. Jesus said, "If anyone wants to be first, he must be . . . the servant of all" (Mark 9:35), and he did *not* add a footnote saying, "except in your home." We discover the happiness God intends for our lives only when we use for the good of another the strengths, resources, and privileges God has given us. By exercising the kind of sacrificial love Christ exhibited, we begin to understand the nature of God's care.

A brown plaster plaque hangs in our home and represents to my wife and me the importance of this sacrificial love. The plaque was an inexpensive wedding present and we received it with little interest, not realizing that we would later come to treasure it. In our early married life of many home and apartment moves, the plaque hung on various walls or was stowed on bookshelves or in kitchen cabinets. Other wedding presents, such as toasters, blenders, and crock pots, eventually gave up the ghost, but somehow the little plaque survived our nomadic existence. It became one of the few constants in our life and before long the plaque came to symbolize home for us. When that plaque was hung on a wall, it was as though we had carved our initials on the house to say, "This is now officially a Chapell home."

What has made us keep that inexpensive wedding gift throughout two decades of marriage is *not* the beauty of its colors or design (it's just a dull brown, round plaque). We have kept it because of the significance of its words: "Home: where each lives for the other, and all live for God." These simple words remind us that our happiness comes from giving ourselves to each other while being obedient to God. Through the years, we have simply sought to live what the words say.

The sacrifice of giving self to the other does not come easily. The various cracks and chips on the plaque remind us that life is full of knocks that threaten the sacrificial unity God intends for us to experience. And the chips that have been repaired are emblems of the deeper reality that when lives are committed to serving one another according to God's Word, then marriage partners can overcome difficulties, and mended marriages can bring enduring joy.

The Questions of Sacrifice

But what does it mean to serve one another in the context of marriage? Is a man to ignore the Bible's instruction to be the spiritual leader in the home? Should a woman be a doormat to her husband's demands? How would either of these choices honor God or help others know his love?

These questions are answered not by discounting what God requires of men and women in the home but by seeing how the duties assigned to each should benefit the other. Biblical leadership means that a man places his family's interests above his own. He uses his leadership to put each member of the family in the best position possible to know and experience the care of God. A woman who submits to such headship is not feeding the selfishness of her spouse but rather is supporting the godly nurture of her entire family. In this way neither spouse abdicates biblical responsibilities but rather fulfills the biblical definition of love that "is not self-seeking" (1 Cor. 13:5).

Widespread misunderstanding of these biblical standards, even among those who are trying to do what God requires, is a consequence both of the well-documented breakdown of the traditional family and also of the tenacious orientation to self that resides in every heart. Both of these factors continually tempt us to dispense with biblical instruction when it does not conform to cultural trends, or to use the Bible selectively so that its standards will serve our own interests. Not only does this departure from Scripture's guidance distance us from the relationships God intends, it also endangers the next generation of families.

Without long-term, Christian models and experience, it is extremely difficult to know at a deep level of one's being what

God expects daily in our homes. Neither teaching individuals more Bible facts nor introducing them to the doctrinal distinctives of a particular church will secure the kinds of families God wants us to enjoy. A young man raised in a legalistic home does not automatically learn how to be a father and husband because he knows the Greek word for each. A woman neglected by her parents throughout her childhood will yearn to know if she is nurturing her own children correctly long after a three-hour seminar on biblical mothering has given her thirty easy steps to disciplining preschoolers.

The Standards of Sacrifice

As the values of our secular society continue to assail our families, it becomes increasingly critical that Christian homes where God's Word is honored have an effective witness for the gospel, ensuring the spiritual well-being of the next generation. Without healthy Christian homes where the unselfish and sacrificial care of Jesus is daily demonstrated, the deep realities of the Christian faith remain mere abstractions to family members and thus fail to take root in society as a whole.

The *Index of Leading Cultural Indicators,* published by the Heritage Foundation, demonstrates well that the practice of living sacrificially for one another is a fading reality for our families. The index shows that over the last three decades in the United States, the marriage rate has declined by half, the divorce rate has more than doubled, the percentage of children with single mothers has nearly tripled, and the percentage of births to unwed mothers has quintupled—accounting for 28 percent of all births.[1] Each statistic in its own way signals a society where satisfying oneself dominates even our most intimate relationships.

The message of Christ's selfless care will not echo in our marriages and families unless we adopt God's values that are radically counter to the me-orientation of the present or the me-Tarzan-you-Jane stereotypes of the past. This book will help those who are genuinely committed to discovering God's plan for caring relationships in their home. In the following pages we will walk through the instruction of key passages in Scripture where the first Christians were told how to organize relationships in their homes. Where this walk leads may surprise some. For although the apostolic writers addressed Christians in a secular culture much like our own, their words did not call the early Christians to retreat from their society. Instead, the apostles called each Christian to retreat from self.

By teaching the sacrifice of one's own priorities to the needs of a loved one, the apostles planned to beacon the truths of Christ's love in a way the world could not ignore. As we live for each other, we reenact the story of Jesus' sacrifice that lifts us from the bottomless pit of self-indulgence to a purposeful life with God.

An example of such sacrificial love surfaced a few years ago in my hometown when two brothers decided to play on sandbanks by the river's edge. Because our town depends on the river for commerce, dredges regularly clear its channels of sand and deposit it in great mounds beside the river. Nothing is more fun for children than playing on these mountainous sandpiles—and few things are more dangerous.

While the sand is still wet from the river's bottom, the dredges dump it on the shore. The piles of sand dry with rigid crusts that often conceal cavernous internal voids, formed by the escaping water. If a child climbs on a mound of sand that has such a hidden void, the external surface easily collapses into the cavern. Sand from higher on the mound then rushes into the void, trapping the child in a sinkhole of loose sand. This is exactly what happened to the two brothers as they raced up one of the larger mounds.

When the boys did not return home at dinnertime, family and neighbors organized a search. They found the younger brother. Only his head and shoulders protruded from the mound. He was unconscious from the pressure of sand on his body. The searchers began digging frantically. When they had cleared the sand to his waist, he roused to consciousness.

"Where is your brother?" the rescuers shouted.

"I'm standing on his shoulders," replied the child.

With the sacrifice of his own life, the older brother had lifted the younger to safety. So too did the one who is not ashamed to call himself our brother, despite our waywardness (Heb. 2:11). We live eternally by standing before God on the righteousness that Jesus Christ provided at the cost of his own life. This is the grace that God extends to us and that we express to others as we use our every resource, gift, and prerogative for the good of another.

In the Christian home each person has the mission of lifting the other to know more of God's care. Greater strength, higher authority, and deeper insight are neither abandoned nor used for the promotion of self, but rather are fully used for the good of the other.

The Mission of Sacrifice

Such exemplary love will not only thrive in our homes, if we submit ourselves to God's Word, it can also change our world. Living as a Christian family in the midst of a godless society has a transforming power of unparalleled spiritual magnitude. Church historians report that Christianity swept the ancient Roman world, not so much because of the arguments of theologians but because of the infectious love evident in Christian families. This spiritual contagion can spread again. As Christ's love changes our families, it also becomes powerfully evident and appealing to outsiders who are desperate for answers to the family decline so frequently reported in our society. The beauty of this societal influence is that it does not merely benefit others. As we model God's grace—his unconditional care for the undeserving—we too understand and experience more of it.

The purpose of this book is to help men and women know how to express God's grace to one another. My goal is not to provide a fix-it recipe for every family problem. Given the complexities of our relationships and situations, I have little confidence in cookie-cutter formulas for happiness. Rather I intend to focus on the foundation principles undergirding the relationships of the

Christian family. My prayer is that once family members examine these principles in Scripture and understand them, they will be able to apply them to the great variety of decisions, routines, and responsibilities required in each home.

Though I am a husband and a father of four, I do not write as an expert who has a ready answer for every situation. My mistakes are more than I can number. Christian family models in my background have often been confusing, and my own heart (true to its human nature) resists sacrifice. The thoughts collected here have resulted from my own need to submit to the teaching of God's Word. As I write, I too am listening for the counsel of Scripture because I recognize that the beauty of my marriage and joy in my family depend on daily application of God's Word to the relationships in our home.

A key Bible passage on which much of this book is based appears below. Although many of the phrases are familiar, they do not always receive a sympathetic hearing in our times. I quote them here as an invitation to each reader to check the words of this book against Scripture. Whether a family has spanned decades or is just beginning, it will only know the fullness of God's love as its members live in obedience to his Word. Thus any human counsel about the responsibilities of Christian men and women should be heeded only to the extent that it conforms to the Bible's teachings on our submission to God and to his standards for mutual care of each other in our homes. This is what God says:

Submit to one another out of reverence for Christ.
Wives, submit to your husbands as to the Lord. For the husband is the head of the wife as Christ is the head of the church, his body, of which he is the Savior. Now as the church submits to Christ, so also wives should submit to their husbands in everything.
Husbands, love your wives, just as Christ loved the church and gave himself up for her to make her holy, cleansing her by the washing with water through the word, and to present her to himself as a radiant church, without stain or wrinkle or any other blemish, but holy and blameless. In this same way, husbands ought to love their wives as their own bodies. He who loves his wife loves himself. After all, no one ever hated his own body, but he feeds and cares for it, just as Christ does the church—for we are mem-

bers of his body. "For this reason a man will leave his father and mother and be united to his wife, and the two will become one flesh." This is a profound mystery—but I am talking about Christ and the church. However, each one of you also must love his wife as he loves himself, and the wife must respect her husband.

Children, obey your parents in the Lord, for this is right. "Honor your father and mother"—which is the first commandment with a promise—"that it may go well with you and that you may enjoy long life on the earth."

Fathers, do not exasperate your children; instead, bring them up in the training and instruction of the Lord.

Ephesians 5:21–6:4

Part 1

The Sacrificial Husband
To Scale the Heights

Husbands, love your wives, just as Christ loved the church and gave himself up for her.

Ephesians 5:25

The day was bone chilling but clear. My brother picked me up at my apartment just as the sun was coming up, and we headed for the tall rocks and clear rivers of the Ozark Mountains. Home for a leave from the Air Force, my brother had promised to take me mountain climbing.

Specially trained to rescue pilots from any terrain in the world, my brother told me not to worry that I had no idea how to scale tall cliffs that soon loomed before us. "Just do what I tell you," he said. Ropes and safety harnesses, spikes and hammers, rope clamps and helmets soon emerged from his duffel, and up we went.

We started on the smaller rocks with gentle slopes. There I learned how to use the rope clamps and spikes, how to ask for more slack or tension on the rope to make my climb, and how to give the same to my partner to enable him to climb with me. I soon learned that the progress either of us made was integrally related to the actions and responses of the other.

By midday I was feeling confident about our routines, and my brother pointed to the sheer face of a cliff across the valley. "Now you're ready," he said. I gulped but agreed.

We hiked to the cliff, roped ourselves together, and side by side we started up. My brother set the course, but I soon discovered this did not always mean that he was above me. The nature of the obstacles and crevices before us meant that sometimes he advanced ahead of me, and sometimes I preceded him. We gave each other tension or slack depending on what was needed to leverage our bodies up the rock. There was no question who was in charge, but neither was there any question that the one who led the way had to let his partner advance with and sometimes ahead of him for us to both make progress.

The goal was not for one to stay on top of the other, but for both to reach the top. To do this, the one in charge had to assess his own strengths and limitations (and those of his partner) and adjust his own actions and directions accordingly. Had he always insisted on being in front regardless of the nature of the challenge, then neither of us would have made the summit.

How these dynamics play out in a marriage as well as on a mountain is the subject of the following chapters. The partners in a biblical marriage are not usually scaling a mountain, but they are always seeking to reach the summit of their godly potential both as individuals and as a couple. The challenges of careers and children, finances and failures, relatives and regrets, make it unlikely that the same person can be out in front all the time if the marriage is to succeed. Thus we need to assess what responsibility marriage partners bear for themselves and for their spouses if their growth in grace is to reach the summit God intends.

one

A Man's Responsibility
Servant Leadership

She steals from him. From the outside they appear to have an ideal home. The house is beautiful, the couple is attractive, and the kids are sweet. Inside things are far from ideal—the wife has a gambling addiction. She has been to counselors, clinics, and pastors. Nothing helps permanently. Periodically she breaks into her own family's bank accounts (or pawns family valuables) and gambles away the money.

Her actions have put her family on the edge of bankruptcy time and time again. The debts accrued cannot be covered even by her husband's executive salary. The financial damage done to the family will take half a lifetime to repair. But the worst damage is not financial, it is relational. Can you imagine your own wife stealing from you, destroying your family's security, and lying about it for months on end?

What should the husband in this marriage do? Consider first what our society tells him to do. It screams, "Get out of that marriage. You don't have to take this. You don't have to put up with her. Leave!"

This husband has not left. Every time his wife has stolen from him and damaged his future, he has forgiven her and taken her back. Even when she was ready to kill herself—ready to give up on her own life—he has loved her. Like the biblical prophet Hosea who took back his unfaithful wife, Gomer, my friend has accepted his wife, despite her failures, over and over.

Once I asked this young man why he had not ended this nightmare marriage. His words were as courageous as they were simple. He said, "My wife is a good mother most of the time. My children need her. But more than that they need to know their Savior. How can they know of a Father in heaven who forgives them if their father on earth will not forgive their own mother? How can my wife know the love of God if the spiritual leader in this home will not love her despite her faults?"

In Christ's name and out of concern for the spiritual good of his family, the man holds on to his marriage. There is nothing more important to him than that his children and wife are spared a hell greater than his own. His chief priority is that his family would know God's eternal grace. Thus the husband takes every precaution to keep funds from his wife that will feed her weakness, he insists on continued counsel, he entrusts her with responsibilities that will boost her self-image, he ensures the regular church attendance of his family, he treats his wife with respect before others, and he loves her.

He uses every means at his disposal, every fiber of his strength, every aspect of his biblical authority, and every commitment of his heart to help his wife. In these ways he fulfills his biblical responsibility to be the head of his home even as he sacrifices himself for the good of those he loves.

The Head of the Home

Though the situation described may seem atypical, the husband's conduct exemplifies the responsibility to which God calls all men in Christian marriage. The husband looks past his own rights to consider what is right for his spouse. He then refuses to surrender his leadership role in the family, but rather uses his biblical authority to arrange the family's resources and activities to serve the best interests of his wife and children.

The apostle Paul articulates this complex responsibility to which God calls Christian husbands through an initially perplexing *tension* evident in his classic New Testament passage on family relationships. Paul first urges all Christians to "submit to one another" (Eph. 5:21). Then, immediately following this general command for submission to one another, the apostle specifically tells wives to "submit to [their] husbands" because "the husband is the head of the wife" (5:22–23).[1]

At first glance the apparent call for mutual submission followed by the announcement that the man is the head of the wife, seems to echo George Orwell's infamous line in *Animal Farm* that "all animals are equal but some animals are more equal than others." How can we be in submission to one another when someone is head over the other? Trouble brews around this word *head*. Our culture and our consciences demand that we determine both what the term means and what it requires.

There are those in our day who try to dismiss concerns about this difficult term by claiming that the concept of headship, which Paul advocates, is either: (1) subject to his own chauvinism or (2) specific to Paul's culture.

Was Paul a Chauvinist?

We cannot accept the first claim—which simply asserts that Paul erred due to his male prejudices—without undermining the authority of all Scripture, which claims to be the inspired Word of God (2 Tim. 3:16; 2 Peter 1:20–21). If the apostles were actually writing their own fallible opinions, while claiming that God had provided them (1 Thess. 2:13; 2 Peter 3:15–16), then the Bible's writers were either terribly deluded or inexcusably deceitful. Either alternative would deny us confidence in anything they wrote and would leave us with only our own opinions to judge what parts of Scripture we will allow to instruct us. The result of such reasoning is that we would become the judges of the Bible, rather than allowing the Bible to judge our actions. Thus our preferences would determine what the Bible says, and we would assume the role of God. Knowing my own sin and limited understanding, this is not a role I want to assume.

Rather than taking the divine prerogative of picking and choosing what passages of the Bible I want to heed, I am content to listen to the Bible's own counsel not to add to or subtract from its instruction (Deut. 4:2; Gal. 1:8; Rev. 22:18–19). In this way God's Word remains intact, and I can continue to rely on wisdom greater than my own.

Was Paul's Culture Alone Addressed?

The second claim, that Paul's standards for the relationship of men and women applied only to his specific cultural situation, needs serious consideration. There surely are times that the apostle gives instructions limited to his ancient culture. When Paul encourages all Christians to greet one another with a holy kiss (1 Thess. 5:26) and when he instructs women to wear head coverings in worship (1 Cor. 11:6) he does *seem* to be referring to cultural practices of his day. I stress the word *seem*, because Christians may seriously differ over the degree to which they feel these practices still apply.

It can be very difficult to decide how to apply ancient practices, such as the Old Testament instruction to leave the edges of one's fields unharvested so that strangers and the poor in the land can find food (Lev. 19:9–10). It is not nearly so difficult, however, to discern the abiding principles behind the practices. The edges of fields were to be left unharvested so that God's people would show compassion for the needy. A holy kiss was to be exchanged among all in the church so that favoritism would be shunned and fellowship would be enhanced.

Head coverings also communicated abiding principles but not in signals that we understand today. A woman in the ancient world wore a head covering to signify that she was under the authority of another. By contrast a man did not cover his head to show that he was under the authority of God (1 Cor. 11:3–4).[2] These cultural cues were used to communicate biblical principles of authority in the New Testament churches but the cues no longer communicate the same thing, making their continued practice meaningless.[3] The loss of meaning of the practices, however, does not mean the principles of authority are not still in effect. In the same passage where Paul speaks of head covering he says, "the head of every man is Christ, and the head of the woman is man, and the head of Christ is God" (v. 3). The fact that what we wear on our head and why has changed over time does not mean that a man is no longer under the authority of Christ, nor that Christ is no longer under the authority of God—nor that a woman's relationship to her husband has changed.

More will be said in part 2 of this book about the ways in which the apostles emphasize the universal and perpetual nature of their principles for the way men and women should relate in families. For the moment, we need only to recognize that in his Ephesian letter, where Paul details the headship responsibility of men in families, the apostle also establishes the nature of the church in both its macro and micro components. If what he says about such basic relationships between men and women is false for our times, then we have no reason to think that any principles he gives for organizing our homes and churches continue to conform to God's plan.

The uncertainty to which such a conclusion enslaves us is all the more apparent when we recall that Paul says that "the husband *is* the head of the wife as Christ *is* the head of the church" (Eph. 5:23, italics mine). This powerful comparison makes it apparent that if the husband *is* no longer head of the wife, then the headship of Christ over his church *is* also now uncertain.[4] The impact of such an uncertainty would be nothing short of despair for all Christians, and it cautions us against cavalier dismissal of the principles of authority the New Testament establishes for men and women.

The apostles intended their instructions to Christian families to have continuing relevance for us. This means that the headship principle is valid for today. The chief task I assume here is not to *defend* the present application of the principle but to *define* its perpetual meaning.

What Headship Isn't

We can begin to understand what this word *head* (*kephale* is the original Greek term) means in home relationships by ruling out some possibilities.

First, being the "head" of a home does *not* mean *nothing.* By saying that Christ is *head* of the church (Eph. 5:23), the apostle Paul underscores the importance of the headship concept. We cannot simply disregard the term when it helps define who Jesus is. Christ's identification as a head gives significance to the word and clarifies its meaning.

Ignoring Responsibility

The Bible says that as the head of his bride, the church, Christ serves as her Savior (Eph. 5:23). Jesus gave himself out of love to make the church holy, radiant, and blameless (5:25–27). Christ's example shows that headship involves taking responsibility—even to the point of personal sacrifice—for the well-being of another. Such a definition grants nobility to the phrase "being a man" and renders boyish and undeveloped those images of manliness that idealize personal independence, family disinterest, and a "sportin' life." The Marlboro man and Michelob weekends represent true manhood about as well as a five year old in a cowboy hat resembles John Wayne.

The strength of character and quality of heart required to head a home for one's adult lifetime make a masculinity that is defined as only taking care of self seem like Milquetoast. As a child I witnessed true manhood in my father, whose job required that he frequently be on the road. The company for which my father worked provided a standard travel stipend based on the distance his travels took him from home. The stipends could have provided fine hotel rooms and meals that would have made my father's trips quite pleasant. But rather than take advantage of the business perks, my father would drive many hours late at night to get home and be at breakfast when his children awoke for school the next morning. Even then his sacrifice was not done.

Not only did my father give of himself to be with his family, but he also gave away the money that he saved by coming home so late at night. For many years the extra money has been placed into a special bank account to provide for the future of my younger brother, whose learning disabilities will limit his independence. My father took seriously his responsibility as head of the home and he was willing to sacrifice to fulfill it.

Excusing Passivity

The biblical head of a family selflessly acts on behalf of those God has committed to his care. This description of headship repudiates modern perspectives that make headship a nasty synonym for self-seeking power plays. More important, because the term describes Christ's agonizing efforts for those he loves, we know that men who use headship as an excuse for passivity in their marriage are wrong. Those husbands who will not expend the effort to do anything responsible in their homes may claim they are exercising the prerogatives of headship, but in reality they are abandoning their biblical responsibilities.

A mother of three recently told my wife, "My husband hasn't made a decision regarding our family in two years. He makes no attempt to discipline the children—that's left to me. He never consults me about taking out-of-town work assignments. He comes and goes seemingly without any regard for my feelings or our children's needs. They don't even know him. All he does is come home from time to time and break our routine before leaving again. I don't have three children—I have four."

This wife complains frequently to her husband about his habits, and he tells her that in a few weeks he will work out a time when they can talk about it. But he never does. He is a man whose headship is defined by passivity. His headship really means nothing but taking care of himself.

Popular media and feminist objectors to biblical statements about headship frequently accuse the apostles of endorsing male dictatorships, but my experience as a pastor and counselor is that wives are as frequently distressed by their husbands' disinterest. Especially in troubled marriages, men seem to have a passive disregard for their families. In such homes the woman (typically the more verbal one) may constantly complain to the husband about what he is not doing. To keep himself from being psychically or physically disturbed, the man reacts to the verbal pressure by erecting a shell of nonresponsiveness or by immersing himself in interests that insulate him from home concerns. All the while the man may convince himself that because the Bible makes him the head of his home, he has the right to be involved as little as he pleases.

A husband's passivity can actually establish behaviors that lead to an abusive relationship. A common pattern in abusive marriages is long periods of male passivity interspersed with brief episodes of rage. During the periods of relative calm, the man may respond minimally to his wife's complaints. As a result the wife may be encouraged to needle her husband more to get further cooperation, but his responsiveness often comes at a high price. Even when he complies with the wishes of his wife, the words that shame him into action may still steam inside him like an emotional pressure cooker that appears unperturbed from the outside but is actually about to explode. The placid exterior of the husband camouflages the mental or emotional stockpile of grievances and offenses that he perceives have destroyed his personal peace.

When the explosion occurs, the man briefly asserts himself with intense aggression. He may later view the abuse as untypical of himself and, therefore, will feel guilty and willing to apologize. However, this sense of shame will be a further reason for the husband to distance his actions and emotions from the marriage, causing him to return to the nonresponsiveness that elicits more verbal needling from his wife and sets up the abuse cycle to repeat.

Headship that is used as an excuse for abuse or for family disregard has no biblical support. Men who have made idols of the cultural icons of swaggering independence and managerial machismo program their actions and emotions to be self-absorbed, self-contained, and nonresponsive. They define their family role by what they have a right *not* to do. Being a biblical head of a home demands more than passive avoidance of whatever is bothersome, disquieting, or irksome. Indifference to the needs of one's family is not biblical headship. Contrary to the teachings prevalent in both Christian and secular settings, God requires the *active* sacrifice of the head of a home. Biblical headship does not mean nothing.

Imposing Inaccurate Definitions

Biblical headship must mean something. However, just as we cannot ignore Scripture and define headship in ways that excuse self-centered living, we should not impose definitions that the Bible will not support.

Source

It may be less offensive to modern sensibilities if we define the term *head* to mean something like "source" or "origin." In our English usage *head* sometimes means source, as when we refer to the headwaters of a river. Were we to use this definition to determine what the Bible means when it says, "the husband is the head of the wife" (Eph. 5:23), we might decide that it means only that the man—in the person of Adam from whose rib his Eve was formed—preceded his wife in creation (see Genesis 2:21–23).

By applying this logic to the language of the apostles, some have argued that the Bible does not say that a husband has any leadership responsibilities in the home greater than those of his wife.[5] Passages dealing with headship are interpreted to say that since woman came from man, man is merely the source of woman. Such interpretations enable us to avoid having anyone in authority over anyone else and fit well with current trends that minimize the differences between men and women.

The problem is that *head* does *not* merely mean source in the Bible.[6] When New Testament scholar Wayne Grudem catalogued the 2,336 instances of the use of this term in ancient Greek literature, he could find no clear instances where the word exclusively carried the idea of source or origin.[7] Further, the context of the passages where man is described as the head of the home makes it clear that the term refers to some kind of authority.[8] After all, wives are told to submit to their husbands because man is the head of the wife, even as the church is to submit to Christ because he is her head (see Eph. 1:10, 22; 5:22–24; 1 Cor. 11:3, 10). Even if *head* were only to mean "source" in the Bible,[9] most contemporary readers will recognize that it hardly offends modern sensibilities any less for the Bible to say that man is the source of woman. Changing the meaning of *head* to source really solves nothing.[10]

Superiority

Just as wrong as underrepresenting the authority implicit in biblical headship, is overstating it. Some husbands use their headship designation as justification for making personal slaves of their wives. One of the horrors of my early pastoral experience was dealing with a man who believed the Bible supported his right to torture his wife with a cigarette lighter if she did not submit to his sexual desires. Another man made his wife log the hours she did housework to make sure she did not loaf while he was at work. Of such men Kent Hughes appropriately writes:

> God's Word in the hands of a religious fool can do immense harm. I have seen "couch potatoes" who order their wives and children around like the grand sultan of Morocco—adulterous misogynists with the domestic ethics of "Jabba the Hut" who cow their wives around with Bible verses about submission—insecure men whose wives do not dare go to the grocery without permission, who even tell their wives how to dress. But the fact that evil, disordered men have perverted God's Word is no reason to throw it out.[11]

The Bible requires men to treat their wives with consideration and respect (1 Peter 3:7). Headship does *not* grant spiritual or personal superiority to husbands that allows them to inflict arbitrary, selfish, prideful, or capricious rule on their spouses. This should be clear from the apostle's words: "Husbands, love your wives" (Eph. 5:25). The Bible says, "Love is patient, love is kind. It does not envy, it does not boast, it is not proud. It is not rude, it is not self-seeking, it is not easily angered, it keeps no record of wrongs" (1 Cor. 13:4–5).

Nowhere does Scripture define love—even for the heads of households—as taking advantage of others for personal gain. The apostle's command for husbands to love their wives rules out any definition of headship that allows or encourages using or harming others. This is more than clear in the example Paul gives to instruct husbands how they should love. He writes that husbands should love their wives "just as Christ loved the church and gave himself up for her" (Eph. 5:25). This should call to mind Jesus' sacrificial ministry: the washing of feet, the giving up of heavenly glory, the suffering on a cross. Biblical headship never permits using one's position or power over another for selfish benefit.

What Headship Is

Defining headship by saying what it isn't does not answer all the questions that our society or our hearts have. We need to know what biblical headship involves. What does the Bible mean when it says that the husband is the head of the wife?

Possessing Authority to Lead

The head of a home *possesses the most authority* in the family. The conclusion that God grants this authority to husbands is difficult to sidestep when we read what the Bible plainly says. The apostle Paul instructs wives: "submit to your husbands" (Eph. 5:22). Then he gives the *reason* for this submission: "the husband is the head of the wife" (v. 23). Next he offers an *example* of what this submission means: "the husband is the head of the wife as Christ is the head of the church," and "as the church submits to Christ, so also wives should submit to their husbands" (vv. 23–24). Finally,

Paul indicates the *extent* of this authority: "wives should submit to their husbands in everything" (v. 24).

The instruction to submit to one's husband, combined with the reason given, the example offered, and the extent indicated, clearly communicates that the apostle wants the husband to have primary authority in the marriage (see Titus 2:5; 1 Cor. 11:3–10).

The husband's authority to lead the household, however, does not grant him a right to arbitrary, capricious, or selfish control of his family. Headship has strings attached. The apostle says that just as the church submits to the headship of Christ, so also wives should submit to the headship of their husbands (Eph. 5:22–23). This comparison is important because it limits the authority of a husband's headship as well as legitimizing it.

Because the husband's headship is built on the analogy of Christ's relationship to the church, the right to exercise family authority exists only when the exercise is consistent with Christ's nature and purposes. This does not mean that a wife is only to honor the authority of a husband who is a Christian (see 1 Peter 3:1). The relationship between a husband and wife is rooted in the way God created us to live, and his standards for this relationship do not disappear because our marriages are faulty. Rather, the right ordering of our marriages is one of the ways God brings the beauty of his love into scarred lives. Headship—even flawed headship—is designed to fulfill God's purposes and should be honored accordingly. However, when a husband uses the power of his position to counter the purposes of God, then the man has no biblical authority for those specific wrong actions. The husband who demands that his wife stay in a corner while he abuses their children speaks without biblical authority. Headship that transgresses the purposes of God loses God's endorsement.

A wife's obligation to submit to her husband's authority also has no biblical support when he demands that she disobey God. When Paul tells wives to submit to their husbands as to the Lord in everything, he is not teaching that wives are to treat their husbands as divine. Such homage is due God alone (however much men may wish it otherwise). The command to submit "as to the Lord" (Eph. 5:22) reminds women that their actions ultimately honor God and are accountable to him—in the same way that the

Bible urges us all to work as though we are serving the Lord when we labor for human employers (Eph. 6:5; Col. 3:23). In so honoring employers, we do not make them gods, nor do we feel bound to obey them when they order us to break God's law. In the same way a wife who submits to her husband's authority honors God, but not if by obeying the man, she disobeys God. The wife should submit to her husband "in everything" that God's Word approves.

Husband and wife bear mutual responsibility to obey God. Neither can say that he or she has a right or a requirement to disregard God's standards because of what the other has commanded or neglected. When couples forget these basic principles of Christian living, great harm results. Far into his adult years, a friend I will call Joshua bears the scars of parents who neglected these principles. Joshua grew up in a major eastern city where his father worked the late shift as a taxi driver. Though he rarely woke from his daytime sleep to show any interest in the family, the father would occasionally assert his "spiritual authority" when he returned from work drunk. In those predawn hours the father would awaken his wife and children with threats and beatings in order to "preach the Bible" to them for hours in the living room. To this day Joshua reports that his mother defends his father's actions because, "He is the head of the home, and the Bible says we must submit to his wishes."

I will not claim to have an easy answer for what this long-suffering wife should have done. What I see in her son, however, is a lifetime of family and psychological turmoil over the perverted definition of headship that a husband portrayed and a wife defended. Having been taught that headship included the right to abuse, Joshua became an abuser of his own wife and children until he confronted what Scripture really teaches. The Bible never sanctions the actions of a bully in the name of headship and never approves the abuse of any family member for the sake of submission.

Headship receives biblical sanction and support only when it is governed by godly purposes and practices.[12] The authority God grants husbands, combined with the limitations he places on their exercise of that authority, yields a definition of biblical headship that is far from the patterns of dictatorial rule or disengaged priv-

33

ilege some men want the Bible to justify. *Biblical headship is the conscientious and loving use of the authority God grants a husband to ensure that a home (and all its members) honor God and experience his blessings.*

Using Authority to Serve

Biblical headship assumes responsibility for others. The head of a home *must use his authority to serve* the good of his family. In this sense, biblical headship requires service. The authority the husband possesses must advance purposes greater than self-interest. Paul makes this clear in the way he writes his instructions to husbands and wives. These standards for husbands and wives follow one long sentence in the Greek text that includes instructions for everyone in the church (Eph. 5:18–21). In this extended sentence Paul first urges all persons in the church to be "filled with the Spirit" (v. 18). Then he explains what being filled with the Spirit means. Everyone should: (1) "speak to one another with psalms, hymns and spiritual songs"; (2) "sing and make music in your heart"; (3) "always giving thanks to God"; and (4) "submit to one another out of reverence for Christ" (vv. 19–21). This fourth command for "Spirit-filled" living introduces Paul's instructions for how all are to serve sacrificially in the church family.[13]

To flesh out the nature of the service we should offer one another, Paul deals in succession with three groups of people in the church: wives and husbands, children and parents, slaves (better translated "servants"; see discussion on pages 161–62) and masters. Note that in each grouping the first individuals the apostle mentions (i.e., wives, children, and servants) are those that his culture would already consider to be in a submissive role. In our time instructions with similar impact might tell soldiers to obey their officers—conduct that we already consider proper. The apostle says nothing particularly unsettling for his culture when he tells these individuals to continue to submit—although he does add "reverence for Christ" as a new motive for their submission (5:21).

What should rouse our curiosity and underscore the special nature of Paul's instruction is what he says to those who are not in traditionally submissive roles. First, Paul affirms their authority. For example, the apostle still gives parents authority over children (Eph. 6:1–4), and servants are not encouraged to take a vote to decide whether to obey their masters (6:5–8). Yet despite his refusal to annul the authority of those that his culture considered to be in charge, the apostle will *not* affirm the status quo. He requires people with authority (as well as those in submissive roles) to live sacrificially for the ones God places in their spiritual context and care (cf. 5:1–2, 21, 25).[14]

Paul does not release from obedience those in traditionally submissive roles, nor does he invalidate the roles of those with authority. Instead, he tells *all* parties to place themselves under a biblical mandate to surrender their personal interests to the good of others (5:2). The apostle's words are particularly weighty for those who have authority because they are the ones with the most learning and adjusting to do in the social order that the Bible establishes. Parents must learn how to exercise their authority, while serving the good of their children. Masters now have the responsibility to care for those who work for them. Heads of homes must think of spouse and family before self.

Paul does not remove authority from the heads of homes, he redefines it. Their authority is not the right to order others around for personal benefit; it is the responsibility to arrange for a family's well-being. Biblical authority seeks the good of others and, therefore, serves their best interests. In this sense, the head of a home sacrifices himself for the good of his family and surrenders his desires to the needs of others in the home.

Such standards exhibit the radical nature of New Testament relationships. The Bible cuts across cultural expectations that would keep one group of persons pawns of another. Slicing away at traditional notions of authority, the Bible establishes the responsibilities of a servant/leader—one whose authority is dedicated and directed toward providing for the good of others.[15]

Those who perceive headship as synonymous with dictatorship will have trouble understanding this servant/leader role. Clarity comes, however, when we remember that Jesus exemplified what

God expects of persons in this position. Jesus came as our Savior/Lord—totally surrendering himself to our needs though he had absolute authority (Matt. 28:18). Because he who has all authority in heaven and earth came to serve rather than to be served (20:28), we know that sacrifice does not erase authority. Instead, when authority serves the interests of another, it masters the purpose for which God ordained it.

Because a husband's headship reflects the ministry of Christ, we should understand that the head of a home is Christ's chief representative in that home. A wife and children should better know the love of their Savior through the actions and decisions a man makes. The head of the home dispenses Christ's grace into the home, making sure that God's caring standards guide the family and that his unconditional love governs its relationships. This is an immense responsibility—so overwhelming that it requires every man to seek God's aid humbly.

Only by his own close relationship with the Savior and by regular exposure to the mind of God in Scripture will a man know what it means to be the head of a home. A husband must submit his own life to God before he should expect the submission of anyone else. The true head of a home bows before God, asking for help in being the man God desires, interceding for the welfare of the family, and petitioning for daily wisdom that will make God's grace evident in the home. Only when a man has humbled himself in these ways can he stand to give a proper account to God of his headship in the home.

In his "Wedding Sermon from a Prison Cell," Dietrich Bonhoeffer, the German theologian who lost his life opposing Hitler, wrote of such headship. Written in 1943, the words ring true today because they resonate with Scripture:

> Now when the husband is called "the head of the wife," and it goes on to say "as Christ is the head of the church" (Ephesians 5:23), something of the divine splendour is reflected in our earthly relationships, and this reflection we should recognize and honour. The dignity that is here ascribed to the man lies, not in any capacities or qualities of his own, but in the office conferred on him by his marriage. The wife should see her husband clothed in this dignity.

But for him it is a supreme responsibility. As the head, it is he who is responsible for his wife, for their marriage, and for their home. On him falls the care and protection of the family; he represents it to the outside world; he is its mainstay and comfort; he is the master of the house, who exhorts, punishes, helps, and comforts, and stands for it before God.[16]

The head of a home stands before God on behalf of his family and he lives before his family on behalf of God. This is the only headship God honors.

two

God's Reasons
for Servant Leadership

Written more than one hundred years ago, it has become the most famous love letter of our generation. When the narrator first read the correspondence of a Union soldier on Ken Burns's epic television series, *The Civil War*, the producer was unprepared for the public response. Thousands of requests poured in asking for a transcript of the letter, scores of newspapers around the country reprinted the text, framed plaques and needlepoint of the letter filled craft store windows, wedding presents carried quotations of the letter, and families began to do research to see if they could be related to the loving couple of the century-old correspondence.

The letter that caused such a stir was written by Major Sullivan Ballou to his wife, Sarah, a week before the first battle of Bull Run:

July 14, 1861
Camp Clark, Washington

My very dear Sarah,
   The indications are very strong that we shall move in a few days—perhaps tomorrow. Lest I should not be able to write again,

I feel impelled to write a few lines that may fall under your eye when I shall be no more. . . .

I have no misgivings about, or lack of confidence in the cause in which I am engaged, and my courage does not halt or falter. I know . . . how great a debt we owe to those who went before us through the blood and sufferings of the Revolution. And I am willing—perfectly willing . . . to help maintain this Government, and to pay that debt. . . .

Sarah my love for you is deathless, it seems to bind me with mighty cables that nothing but Omnipotence could break; and yet my love of Country comes over me like a strong wind and bears me unresistibly on with all these chains to the battle field.

The memories of the blissful moments I have spent with you come creeping over me, and I feel most gratified to God and to you that I have enjoyed them so long. And hard it is for me to give them up and burn to ashes the hopes of future years, when, God willing, we might still have lived and loved together, and seen our sons grown up to honorable manhood, around us. I have, I know, but few and small claims upon Divine Providence, but something whispers to me—perhaps it is the wafted prayer of my little Edgar, that I shall return to my loved ones unharmed. If I do not my dear Sarah, never forget how much I love you, and when my last breath escapes me on the battle field, it will whisper your name. Forgive my many faults, and the many pains I have caused you. How thoughtless and foolish I have often times been! How gladly would I wash out with my tears every little spot upon your happiness. . . .

But, O Sarah! if the dead can come back to this earth and flit unseen around those they loved, I shall always be near you; in the gladdest days and in the darkest nights . . . *always, always,* and if there be a soft breeze upon your cheek, it shall be my breath, as the cool air fans your throbbing temple, it shall be my spirit passing by. Sarah do not mourn me dead; think I am gone and wait for thee, for we shall meet again. . . .[1]

Major Ballou was killed at Bull Run.

Why the words of this Civil War soldier live beyond him and so resonate in contemporary hearts bears little mystery. Though the words are not theologically precise, they convey a heart of great courage and compassion. There is no question about the manliness of the one who wrote these words and was willing to fight and die for his country. At the same time, the love he expresses reveals a remarkable tenderness. A man so strong that he can afford to be tender is able to give his wife deep knowledge of her own preciousness. Such a gift is treasured in any age.

The way Major Ballou used his courage and love to give his wife strength and value hints at the purposes God ordains for biblical headship. The servant/leader responsibilities God gives Christian husbands have a redemptive intent. As the head of the church, Jesus sacrificed himself so that his people could know their value to God (cf. Mark 10:45; 2 Cor. 8:9; Titus 2:14). This redeeming work continues through the way God organizes families. Husbands who reflect Christ's headship use their authority as he did, seeking for their wives to know and reflect their preciousness to God.

The head of a home communicates God's love primarily in the way he cares for his family members. Thus the apostle says, "Husbands, love your wives, just as Christ loved the church and gave himself up for her" (Eph. 5:25). Such giving should govern the lifetime goals as well as the daily responsibilities of Christian men. In this way the grace of God, the unearned gift of his love, becomes real to the wife over whom a man has authority.

To Glorify the Wife

The headship that honors Christ brings glory to women. Such husbanding enables a spouse to know God's care for her despite personal imperfections, circumstantial difficulties, and self-doubt. This redemptive purpose to which the husband should submit his efforts is apparent in Paul's description of Christ's care for his bride, the church. The apostle calls men to make this spiritual relationship their model of care as husbands:

> As Christ [the authoritative Lord of the universe] loved the church and gave himself up for her . . . by the washing with water through the word, and to present her to himself as a radiant church. . . . In this same way, husbands ought to love their wives.
>
> Ephesians 5:25–28

41

Our Lord submitted his life to the purpose of glorifying his bride. His goal was to help her realize her eternal preciousness and value, so he purchased, with the price of his own blood, the radiant beauty God desired for his spiritual spouse.

Compare such a purpose to these words a Christian woman recently wrote about the head of her home:

> I hate him. I hate him because he made me feel worthless, inadequate—like a nonperson, a slave. I could never do anything that made him happy. I always came short of the mark. I was always desperately working to win his approval. I hate him for the crummy way he made me feel about myself. I don't know whether I will ever get over the hurt he caused in my life.

We cannot excuse this wife's anger and bitterness, but neither should we seek to justify that type of marital headship that, with the most selective and self-serving of biblical proof texts, ignores its biblical purposes. Instead of making his wife feel precious, this husband's headship made her feel worthless. Christ's love, on which the husband's love is supposed to be modeled, never makes us feel "crummy," "worthless," and "like a nonperson." The authority in this marriage was improperly expressed in that it failed to confirm or to instill in the wife the divine value God purposes for his people. Such unbiblical headship is actually a form of robbery because it takes from a person some measure of the knowledge of grace God intends for her to possess.

Robbing another of his or her sense of value sounds horrible, yet it is extremely common. Whether such robbery is deliberate or not, it is almost always the result of an insecurity that compels a husband to establish his own sense of worth by exerting power or control over his wife. Some evil math in us seems to reason that when we have managed to reduce another's sense of worth, then our own value increases.

My wife, Kathy, is one of the most competent, capable people I know. Her grades were far better than mine in school. For two years straight she was selected as the outstanding musician among all music majors at her university. Numerous academic and professional honors have come her way. Yet after we had been married only a short while, I realized that I had robbed her of a significant amount of her self-worth.

I made this discovery when our washer needed repair. I was busy and asked Kathy to call a repairman while I was at work. She agreed to do so but then did not get around to calling. The next day she again agreed to call the repairman, but when I returned from work, she still had not called.

That evening, when I confronted Kathy for not phoning the repairman, she confessed in tears that she did not feel capable of making the call. We both remember the event vividly. She remembers because that conversation now embarrasses her. I remember because it scared me.

I thought, *Kathy, what is wrong with us that after a year of being married to me, you—so capable and intelligent—think so little of yourself that you cannot make a phone call? How have I managed to reduce you to this? What have I done to you?*

I cannot say that answers came immediately to those questions—neither my thought nor my theology were mature—but I will tell you of an image that regularly flashed into my mind for months after that moment. In my mind's eye I saw a framed print that used to hang in my grandmother's home. The picture shows a young man at the wheel of a great ship during a violent storm. Wind whips the sails into tattered sheets around the boy, and the waves crash about him. Yet despite the great threat and obvious challenge, the boy's face remains calm and confident. The reason is clear. In the picture Jesus is standing behind the young pilot of the ship. The Savior's hand rests on the boy's shoulder, and the caption beneath the picture reads, "Jesus is my copilot." The words and the image communicate that when we sense the presence of the Savior, our confidence grows to meet any challenge.

The opposite was happening in my relationship with my wife. My presence often made her self-confidence vanish. She felt like a capable driver only when I was not in the car. She doubted her competence in social gatherings only when I was in the conversation. In a thousand ways (some of which I recognized and others I did not) I made my wife question her adequacy and thus I robbed her of a sense of her own worth. I had to reexamine myself in the light of Christ's model for the church. My headship should build up my wife, enabling her fully to sense and to live out the reality of the treasure that she is to me and to her Savior. She cannot readily know or reflect her worth to God if the husband he has provided constantly diminishes her. She will not glorify God with the radiance he intends if her husband deprives her of glory.

Since Paul uses Christ's relationship with the church as the model for how husbands should relate to their wives, the descriptions of Jesus' care for his spiritual bride provide important guidance for how Christian husbands should honor their wives.

Communicating Forgiveness

Paul says Jesus cleansed his bride, the church, "by the washing with water through the word" (Eph. 5:26). This reference to the baptism that Christ provided the church to signify the core truth of Scripture that his blood cleanses us from our sin holds important implications for husbands. The gospel of Christ's forgiveness should be a dominant voice in our homes. Initially this means that the message of the Bible should make a daily appearance in our homes through family devotions, church participation, and personal conversation. In the premarital counseling I do, I have been struck by how often young women ask me to impress on their future husbands the importance of family devotional reading. These women sense that the security of their marriages, their value as persons, and their ability to fulfill God's purposes for their lives is enhanced when their husbands are committed to God's Word.

Of course, verbal commitment to the truths of God's forgiveness is a cruel sham if those principles are not lived out. A husband reassures loved ones of God's goodness and of each individual's significance in his sight when—as the head of the home—he consistently reflects the reality of forgiving grace.

When Kathy and I were first married, we lived in a small, rented farmhouse. The twisting roads from our home to our jobs were particularly treacherous in the winter because our rural community did little to clear snow and ice. We had only one compact car between us—all we could afford and our only mode of transportation. During a devastating ice storm, when Kathy was driving, the car slid off the road and into a ditch. Faced with a repair bill, a tow charge, and difficulty now getting to work, I had little mercy on my wife. I explained the need for greater care, I went into detail about how to turn into a skid to get control of a car on ice, and I reminded her that our finances could not handle such "accidents" that a little more skill and caution would avoid. Two days later, I put the car in a ditch.

Fortunately, the ice lasted a little longer and Kathy put the car in a ditch again. Unfortunately, so did I!

Our ice-driving experiences were an important reminder to me that everyone needs forgiveness because everyone makes mistakes. I think the Lord helped me into those ditches because the husband who realizes that he also needs pardon will most effectively communicate God's mercy to his wife.

The healing and health Kathy and I have experienced in our marriage (and seen in others where the problems have been much more serious) relate directly to forgiveness. A husband who grants forgiveness because he knows he also needs forgiveness shows his wife she is valued despite her faults and is not less deserving of mercy than he. As a result, forgiveness communicates the preciousness of a spouse, confirms that the spiritual need of one is no greater than that of the other, and powerfully unites a couple in the knowledge that their weaknesses do not invalidate their love—or God's.

Confirming Beauty

Paul says Christ made the church radiant for himself (Eph. 5:27). He promoted her beauty. I am not saying that we should equate value with physical beauty. Counselors tell us, however, that husbands who make wives question their appearance or who encourage their dowdiness are often trying to control their spouses. By making women question whether others will find them acceptable or attractive, these men seek to isolate their wives emotionally and make them dependent on their spouses' approval.

Controlling others by demeaning them or by making them question their worth is abhorrent to God and contrary to the goals of the gospel. God sent his Son to the cross to demonstrate to us that we are "dearly loved" (5:1–2) and he commands us to say and do only what will build up one another in the knowledge of his care (4:29–32).

God intended marriage partners to be attractive to one another so that their physical union might strengthen the bond of their hearts. One way that we strengthen this bond and build up our spouses is by affirming the physical and personal beauty we cherish in them. We husbands affirm this beauty by our loving words, by showing our wives that we desire them—with an affectionate hug as well as with the caring lovemaking the Bible honors (see Gen. 2:20–24; 1 Cor. 7:4–5; Eph. 5:31; Heb. 13:4)—and by providing the loving support that enhances their attractiveness.

The Bible says Jesus made his bride, the church, radiant to him. Husbands should do the same with their brides. I love to shop for clothes with my wife, not because my tastes are any good but because I enjoy seeing what makes her feel beautiful and being able to tell her so.

I realize many husbands dread this kind of shopping. It not only places them in the women's section of a department store, but it may seem to encourage a practice that has already had frightening effects on the family checking account. Yet, a woman who is confident of her beauty (because her husband so affirms her) may feel less of a need for an inexhaustible supply of frills to make her feel pretty.

We diminish each other and our marriages when we do not communicate the ways in which we see beauty in our spouses. This should be part of our rejoicing in what God has provided.

Prioritizing Partnership

A husband further affirms his wife's value by obeying Scripture's command and giving his union with his wife precedence over other family relationships, even that with his own parents (Eph. 5:31). This instruction does not annul our lifetime respon-

46

sibilities to honor our parents but it places priority on the marriage relationship.

Ann Landers and daytime television talk shows would run out of material if all men were to honor the Bible's hierarchy of relationships. The King James Version of the Bible says that a man shall "leave his father and his mother, and shall cleave unto [or be united with] his wife" (Gen. 2:24). The traditional wedding vows many couples still repeat capture the leaving and cleaving principle. The groom promises his bride to "forsake all others and cleave only unto her." This is more than a caution for in-laws to keep their distance and let the new couple make their own lives together. The couple promises to make their marriage relationship a higher priority than all others. The man who keeps this promise honors his wife and his marriage.

When other relationships take priority over the marriage, pain follows. Every church and home knows of those sad families where a husband or wife lets a parent run (or ruin) their marriage. The woman who simply cannot say no to her mother's interference may be blamed for a marriage's trouble, but the man who will not exercise his authority and insist that the meddling stop is also guilty. Although the case is extreme, my wife and I know of a husband who, after years of suffocating in-law entanglement, required his wife's parents to sign a contract promising to limit their visits, criticisms, phone calls, and out-of-control giving of presents to grandchildren. The pain involved in hammering out the agreement was intense, but prior to the contract the now secure marriage was near rupture.

We are also aware of a young man who could not say no to his mother who cooked him treats, bought him clothes, visited him every Sunday, and used him nearly daily as a handyman. This husband warded off his wife's pleas for attention and her warnings of the mother's manipulations with the excuse, "Mom needs me." So did his wife, and his failure to put her first clearly indicated the value he put on her concerns. The young man now lives two doors from his mother, alone.

When the Bible indicates a relationship as important as that of parents and children must take a backseat to the marriage relationship, then the clear message is that no relationship should challenge the oneness of a husband and wife. A husband who confides more personally in his secretary or a work associate than in his wife damages the oneness God intends for his marriage.[2] A man more dependent on the approval of a close friend (male or female) than on that of his wife commits emotional adultery. A man married to a career, to a computer terminal, to a child's success, to a television screen, or to sporting interests more than to his spouse sins against her. When a husband treasures his wife as God intends, then no relationship will exceed the priority of the marriage bond.

Providing Care

Men indicate how highly they value their spouses by the degree of care they give their wives. Paul says husbands ought to care for their wives as they do for their own bodies (Eph. 5:28). The terms used to describe this care relate to physical provision as well as relational warmth (see v. 29). Thus communicating the esteem in which we hold our spouses precludes using our relationships or our resources selfishly. God mandates that our words and our goods should be used for fostering the well-being of our spouses.

Three decades ago a professor, who now teaches at Covenant Seminary, left the United States to direct an international ministry. His wife went with him, leaving a career she loved—teaching French at a prestigious girls' school. When the family returned to the United States twenty years later, her love for French had not diminished, but the family's savings had. There appeared to be little way for the wife to take the college courses needed to renew her expired teaching credentials.

The husband refused to deny his wife her love. By teaching an overload schedule for extra pay, taking temporary jobs, and avoiding all frills in the family budget, the husband sacrificed himself to give his wife the opportunity to teach again. She earned her degree but then, to the surprise of many, she chose to stay at home to support her husband. His job responsibilities had become so pressing that she felt she needed to be home to support him. Though she still wants to teach, she now sacrifices her desires for the benefit of the one who gave himself for her.

With so much sacrificing going on in this family, you may get the idea that theirs is a fairly morbid home. No way! Christian marriages are supposed to work this way. Students and fellow faculty look forward to visiting this couple's home, because joy radiates from its every corner. Mutual sacrifice led by the head of the home breeds the deepest satisfactions love and life can offer.

At his wedding a husband vows, "All that I am I give to you, and all that I have I share with you." With such words a man promises to sustain, without reservation or concealment, the wife God provided. This promise does not prevent a man from delegating resources and responsibilities in the family according to each member's respective talents and strengths; however, this division of labor should not be an excuse for hidden activities or hoarded treasures. A man who marries with the intention of withholding goods, accounts, or affection from his wife, denies himself the benefits of the united love God designed to build up both partners in the marriage—and such a man ultimately damages himself. Scripture wisely indicates that a man should care for his wife as he does himself; for when he does, his wife's well-being becomes his own.

Cherishing Grace

Scripture's analogy that caring for one's wife should parallel the way a man treats his own body holds particular significance for the heart of a husband. A man remains faithful to his body even when it brings him pain. In fact when his body signals pain, he typically gives it more attention. Everyone understands a husband who is faithful to a spouse when she brings him pleasure. But being faithful beyond pleasure makes sense only to those who cherish Christ's love and through it learn to value a spouse for who she is rather than what she offers.

Jesus sacrificed his body for us when we brought him no pleasure, but only heartache and pain. This is the message of grace: God loved us when there was no human reason to love. He treasured us when we had no esteem for him (see Isa. 53:3; Mal. 3:17). To love your wife when her failures cause your hurt, to cherish

49

her at the very moment you believe that someone else could satisfy you more, shows her God's regard for her and thus is the ultimate expression of her worth.

None of the marriage hints above is more critical than the apostle's decree: "Husbands, love your wives" (Eph. 5:25). Paul attaches no condition to the command. He does not say, "Love your wives because they make you happy," or ". . . when they do what you want," or ". . . as long as they are beautiful to you." The command stands alone. To join it to any reason or cause would be contrary to the character of the God who issued the standard.

God loves us purely as a consequence of the relationship he has established with us, not because of any beauty we possess or any service we could offer. Nothing better communicates this grace of God to our spouses than our unconditional love of them. A husband who cherishes his wife simply because of the relationship they established together before God honors both his God and his wife.

Unconditional appreciation of a wife powerfully communicates the grace of God and enables a spouse to experience more fully the glory of God's regard for her. Only when a wife knows this kind of love from a husband do the blessings and passions of mutual affection really have the opportunity to flourish and endure.

I recognize that some reading these words about a husband's headship having the purpose of bringing glory to his wife will feel that this demeans women. The notion that women need men to build them up—as though women somehow are not capable in themselves—can perpetuate horrible stereotypes. Much of what is written in popular Christian literature about men "discipling their wives," being considerate of their "weaknesses," and "tolerating their hormones" is demeaning *and* wrong. The fact that God uses husbands to glorify wives should be qualified by the recognition that, biblically, neither men nor women (except those gifted for celibacy)[3] are complete without their spouses. Thus biblical headship is designed not only for glorifying the wife but also for the redemptive purpose of making the husband all that God intends.

To Complete the Husband

What does God intend for husbands to be? Complete—as emotionally whole and spiritually mature as they can be before they are with him in eternity. But how will this completion come about? Paul says a man "will leave his father and mother and be united to his wife, and the two will become one flesh" (Eph. 5:31). This is more than a reference to the physical union of a man and woman in marriage. The language puts before us the Lord's creation plan to make us whole persons. God created the wife to complement and complete the husband (Gen. 2:20–24). Lest this sound demeaning of her, think of what it connotes for him. The man is ever incomplete, incapable of realizing the divine potential God intends for him in this life, apart from the ministry of his wife in his marriage.

A Union Man

Because two people who marry are to be one, if either party damages, demoralizes, or degrades the other, then neither will be completely whole. Just as a basketball deflated on only one side still cannot fulfill its purposes, so a marriage with one side diminished will deprive both persons of fully being and doing what God desires. God has designed the similarities and differences of a man and woman in marriage to complement and support the spiritual growth of both. Neither party to the marriage can develop fully if either one is denied his or her personal potential.

The man who thinks he will do just fine, regardless of his unwillingness or inability to build up his wife, fools and damages himself. By divine decree husbands and wives are united in mind, spirit, and body. God knits together their personalities and expects them to care for each other. If a man takes advantage of his spouse or robs her of some essential need, then he stunts his own growth as well as hers.

A few years ago my wife and I lived in an apartment complex among students training for ministry. One evening we invited a couple over to our house to play table games. As we were playing a game that requires animated conversation, we realized the guest wife was not really participating. In fact she was playing so miserably that the situation became rather awkward. She would hardly speak up.

When the social tension became intolerable, the husband finally explained to us that the reason his wife was not speaking was that he had recently been embarrassed by things she had said in the company of others. As a result, they had agreed that since he was the head of the house, she should not speak in public unless he granted her permission. They were serious about this! and consequently did not win any of our games that night.

Not surprisingly, of course, there were other problems in this marriage. Some months after the game episode, the husband began to suffer from severe depression and left the seminary. I have never heard from the couple again. Still, I have occasionally speculated on what this man did to himself. The Lord had provided him with a wonderful spouse. Yet by manipulation and intimidation, he had so weakened her that when he needed her support, she was incapable of helping him.

The purpose of a man's headship is not fundamentally different than that of Christ's redemptive activity on behalf of the church. The husband is to be an instrument and channel of God's goodness in his wife's life. As Christ enables each of us to use our personalities and gifts to bring glory to God, so proper headship builds up the wife in such a way that she can bring glory to God. This does not occur when a man makes his wife feel inadequate, incompetent, or incapable. Not only does that kind of headship rob God of the glory he intends for a wife to bring heaven, it can also rob the husband of God's help in time of need. God designed the woman in such a way that her husband can lean on her for support. But if she has been robbed of her self-confidence and cannot stand, she will be of little aid to him.

Husbands who admire (or are jealous for) the strong women they see in other men's marriages intuitively recognize that such wives enable their husbands to fulfill their greatest potential. What men with such a longing may not realize is that they play a large part in making their wives strong. The regard husbands give their wives may largely determine whether such strength of character will emerge in their own marriages.

A Real Man

Husbands require the support and influence of wives. The more capable the wife, the stronger and more appropriate will be her aid. The man who understands this divine design for his own development delights to build up the woman who makes him more able to be what God wants. He recognizes that the regard he gives his wife defines and develops him. Real men respect women.

If husbands will not commit themselves to their wives' growth and good, then the men are diminished. Men were designed to be made whole through the full expression of their spouses' gifts and abilities. When people lack this understanding, many suffer.

Church officials across this nation have recently expressed alarm that so many students who are training for ministry have had such poor family models as a consequence of the pervasive breakdown of American family life. When these students become pastors, they may well know where in the Bible it tells how to deal with other people or even with one's own family, but actually living these words is extremely difficult with the baggage of a difficult childhood. A childhood of pain can render an adult socially awkward, unsure of how to share feelings, incapable of showing affection, and unwilling to develop the deep relationships that require new vulnerability to pain.

A minister close to my family counts himself among those scarred by a childhood in a dysfunctional family. Yet he recently wrote how—through his wife—God had taught him to share more of himself and to be more real with those committed to his care:

> So much of what I had to learn from my wife, after being in a home of constant tension, was simply what it meant to be caring and expressive. In so many ways my wife helped me find *me* when I got married. I did not know how to express affection. I did not know how to express appreciation. I was out of touch with my emotions, having forgotten how to laugh or how to cry. Yet I was

trying to be a minister of the gospel. I dread thinking of what my "ministry" would be if the Lord had not taught me much through the spouse he provided.

Of course being inexpressive or out of touch with one's own feelings is not a problem limited to contemporary pastors. The man who wrote the above is not the first to realize that his wife had much to teach him about caring for others. I am by nature reserved and inexpressive. I recognize that I have had to learn much from my wife about expressing love and affection, even to be able to tell my children how I really feel about them. Without her patient drawing me out of myself over many years, I dread to consider the kind of father, husband, and pastor I would be. Even now I struggle to be as expressive as some of the people around me need. I still have much to learn but I recognize that where I am, what I have done, and the joys I know in career, family, and ministry result directly from my wife's helping me share more of myself with her and others.

A Godly Man

The influence a husband's headship has on his relationships with others should remind us that there are spiritual implications for the way a man expresses his authority. These spiritual aspects of headship obviously relate to whether a man uses his authority for self or others, wrongly or rightly, cruelly or sacrificially. A husband who berates his wife and beats his children may claim that biblical principles of headship support his authority. His actions, however, indicate he has denied the authority of God over his own life. Biblical headship requires a constant examination of one's actions, attitudes, and priorities to see whether they conform to Scripture.

A further, and deeper, understanding of how headship affects one's relationship with God flows from reflection on how a wife's completion of her spouse affects his spiritual health. In a profound way, a wife not only helps a husband find himself, she helps him find the deeper dimensions of his God. This is because the intimate is closely connected to the transcendent. The ability to express and experience human affection opens the door to understanding God's love, even as knowing his love transforms our affections and homes. If you cannot share your heart with persons God has placed in your life, then it is nearly impossible to know how to have an intimate relationship with your Lord. The union of human hearts deepens our understanding of who God is by introducing us to the feelings, actions, and forgiveness God treasures. Thus the kind of headship that damages this union threatens our knowledge of God, just as the headship that promotes the union further reveals him to each of the marriage partners.

The early church father Tertullian wrote of the connection of Christ's love to the marriage relationship:

> How beautiful, then, the marriage of two Christians, two who are one in home, one in desire, one in the way of life they follow, one in the religion they practice. . . . Nothing divides them either in flesh or in spirit. . . . They pray together, they worship together, they fast together; instructing one another, encouraging one another, strengthening one another. Side by side they visit God's church and partake of God's banquet; side by side they face difficulties and persecution, share their consolations. They have no secrets from one another; they never shun each other's company; they never bring sorrow to each other's hearts. . . . [S]eeing this Christ rejoices. To such as these He gives His peace. Where there are two together, there also He is present.[4]

Through the analogies of human affection we gain insight into the divine heart (see 1 John 4:20). By her love and patience my wife has made me more spiritually whole than I could be apart from her. I did not know the ways that I failed to understand God until she opened in my heart doors and depths of love I did not realize existed. I have much still to learn from her. If I had continued to intimidate, not appreciate, and belittle her, then I would never have found the ways I have learned to love. I would have lost parts of myself. Further, in losing those aspects of myself, I would have lost dimensions in which to fathom "how wide and long and high and deep is the love of Christ" (Eph. 3:18).

In the relationships God provides to help make us whole, we discover more of the pervading presence, care, and peace of our Savior. I praise God for the great grace of opening and maturing my heart through my wife's influence. I am thankful for the Word that reminds me that if I do not build her up, then I diminish myself. My sanctification, my wholeness before God, cannot be complete without my honoring Kathy. No wonder the apostle Paul says that the one who loves his wife loves himself (5:28–29, 31). By building up his wife, a man enriches his own life.

As a husband's authority is used to nurture his wife, his own spiritual health is enhanced and he experiences fulfillment. Somewhere buried deep in all of us is the acknowledgment of this truth. By excavating our most private attitudes toward those we know, we discover that our hearts confirm what Scripture attests. We will recognize that men who respect and cherish their wives are typically whole people. Conversely, we will see that those whose view or practice of headship diminishes or de-spirits their wives are husbands who are often emotionally and relationally unhealthy on other fronts as well.

We have all probably known men in business, or even in the church, who are highly respected for their abilities on the job but whose home lives (hidden deep beneath the public facade that wives may also be desperate to protect) disclose a headship of authoritarian rule or self-interested abandonment. Families of such men bear the scars of their heads' stardom even though the work of these men may prosper in the spotlight for many years.

Such men typically substitute career success for family fulfillment. Members of their families and people in the organizations these men lead become mere cogs in the machinery of the men's careers. These men increasingly isolate themselves from feelings for others and have little care for anything other than their own image. They become puppets controlled by their own need for power—a parody of success without fulfillment. Such men disappoint us when we meet them because we expect their success to have brought them more happiness and to have made them more complete and humane persons. Anticipation of such prospects may actually lie behind our own drivenness because it is easy to believe that the respect of men equates with the regard of God.

Scripture warns against these expectations by placing priority on the way a man heads his family as the means of growing in godliness. If a man will not devote himself to honoring those committed to his care, he depletes the soil in which his own spirit must mature. The men who know the greatest rewards of this life—in terms of familial love, personal pride, and spiritual satisfaction—have invested themselves in wives whose strong support makes their husbands healthy and whole.

In the soft coal mines of southern Illinois, collapse of the mine shafts is a constant threat. For this reason the miners use huge bolts to anchor the ceiling of the coal shaft to solid rock above. The system works as long as the supporting rock is strong. But when the supporting rock is weak, the whole structure collapses. So when a man weakens the wife divinely designed for the husband's support, then he endangers the human and spiritual potential of both partners in the marriage. God has better plans. He mandates the godly headship that strengthens and blesses both husband and wife.

three

God's Resources
for Servant Leadership

Almost a generation ago, in a wonderful article entitled "Husbands, Forget the Heroics!" Karen Howe wrote:

I once heard a Christian minister spend an hour talking on the biblical role of husbands and wives. He spent 59 minutes discussing the woman's need to submit and obey, and one minute summing up the husband's role. It was his grand finale: "Men you must love your wives as Christ loves the church. What does that mean?" Dramatic pause. "It means you must be willing to die for her!" He sat down and colorful images raced through my mind of my husband leaping in front of an oncoming bull or offering himself to cannibals in my stead.

However, in view of the more likely challenges of diapers, dishes, and daily schedule juggling, Howe concluded, "Most women do not want their men to die for them. They want their men to live for them."[1]

The gentle sarcasm aside, Howe makes a worthy point. Saying that biblical headship involves the authority to fulfill God's redemptive purposes for both partners in a marriage does not precisely explain what men should do. Grandiose statements about sacrificing for the good of another can lead to daily inaction when such heroics seem unneeded. How are men to exercise headship daily in their marriage as God intended?

The Bible offers no specific this-is-what-you-are-to-do instruction for husbands regarding the division of household tasks, deciding when to move for whose job, determining who drives or who holds the TV remote control, and so on. Yet by uncovering the resources Scripture gives men to help them carry out their responsibilities, we get a clear picture of what should govern a husband's daily considerations, care, and conduct.

In light of how human authority is usually expressed and enforced, we may expect that God would give husbands power, rules, and armaments to enable them to exercise their authority. But the biblical instruction God gives husbands for fulfilling their role as head of the household is shocking, having nothing to do with power. The primary resources God makes available for our headship involve sacrifice—ours and his.

Self-Sacrifice

A chief resource husbands have for enacting their headship is selflessness. When husbands daily love their wives as Christ loved the church, then sacrifice of self is required.

Robertson McQuilkin, a leader not only of his home but of the evangelical world, was, until 1990, president of Columbia Bible College and Seminary. He resigned from the presidency because his wife, Muriel, afflicted with Alzheimer's disease, needed his care.[2]

During his last two years as president, McQuilkin wrote that it was increasingly difficult to keep Muriel at home. When she was with him, she was content but without him, she became distressed and panic-stricken. Though the walk from their home to the school was a mile round-trip, she often tried to follow him to the office. Seeking him over and over, she sometimes made that trip ten times a day. When he took her shoes off at night, McQuilkin found her feet bloodied from all the walking. Washing her feet prepared him for what most saw as an even more Christ-like act, sacrificing his position to take care of her.

This is leadership by serving another—husbanding by humility, ministering by sacrifice. God calls Christian men to such headship.

Leading by Godly Service

A Christian husband leads through service, through selfless love. He has the primary, biblical responsibility in the home to set by his own sacrifice a spiritual standard through which God will govern the family. What kind of authority is this? There is no quick way of saying it. Too often Christians try to summarize male headship in the home by simply saying that the husband has the last word or is the final authority in decision making. Be glad this abbreviation of responsibilities is not found in the phrases of Scripture because it can cause great damage. Such phraseology could mean that even if the wife

- hates the idea of moving to a distant town,
- doesn't want a particular home,
- thinks a child does not need another after-school activity,
- doesn't like a certain kind of lovemaking,
- disagrees with a husband's method of disciplining children, or
- believes an investment is unwise,

the husband should automatically get his wishes anyway because he is the head of the home and has the final word. Such a concept does not exist among the Bible's definitions for headship. While a husband may need to exercise final authority, he has no biblical right to express it without consideration or care of his family's concerns.

Far from encouraging a husband to exercise his authority for personal privilege, the Bible takes care to direct a Christian man

61

to use his authority for the benefit of his spouse and family. Thus biblical headship shifts the focus of husbanding from taking charge to taking responsibility, and from asserting one's will to submitting one's prerogatives to the good of another.

Leading by Godly Nurture

In the same way a man feeds and cares for his own body, the apostle says the husband should express his love to his wife (Eph. 5:29). The King James Version uses the words *nourish* (to bring to maturity) and *cherish* (to foster with tender care) to describe this care that is to parallel the way that Christ tends the church.

Along with the tenderness implicit in these words, there also resides the concept of causing to grow. As Christ gave himself to foster our spiritual growth, a husband is to take responsibility for fostering the spiritual growth of his wife—helping her reach her godly potential. Through a husband's care, a wife should be allowed and encouraged to develop her gifts and talents so that they bring maximum glory to God.

Christ nurtures the ability of each believer to honor God in two ways—by his past example and by his continuing efforts. By living to glorify God, Jesus provided us with an example of Christian maturity. As we read of Christ's compassion, remember his patience, take strength from his courage, seek to pattern his holiness, and follow his sacrifice, we grow. While husbands will not achieve the perfection of their Savior in this life, their headship obligates them to walk as examples before their families.

By his prayer life, his patience, his meditation on God's Word, his integrity, his commitment to his church, his care for his family, and his love for his wife, a husband fosters the personal and spiritual growth of his spouse. Giving himself as Christ did to setting a godly example for his family, a man leads his bride to honor God. Such giving of self may require much sacrifice.

Far into their elderly years a man in our church nurtured his wife's spiritual growth despite her resistance to his care. Because of some perceived slight by members of the church early in their marriage, the wife refused ever again to attend. Her resentment of the church grew as his attendance remained faithful for decades. Some mornings he walked to church because she had hidden the car keys. One Sunday she cut all the buttons off his church suit to discourage his attendance. His example never wavered. Without anger he cared for her, and without speeches he demonstrated how much he valued his worship of the Savior.

She paid no attention until age made him an invalid and he could no longer walk. His faith did not waver, however, and she finally began to consider what had kept his character and conduct so caring through the many years of her own resentment. From his bed this husband led his wife to an eternal relationship with God. Months later, when a sudden illness caused her to precede him in death, the husband grieved but also rejoiced in the knowledge that he would soon be with her to share a relationship of deeper love than they had known in this life. A lifetime of sacrificial example bore eternal fruit because the head of this home nurtured the soul of his wife without regard for his own happiness or convenience.

The actions that bolstered this man's example should remind us that headship requires continuing effort if it is to nurture spiritual growth. By his Spirit, Christ works in our hearts to cause us to grow in his ways. He listens to our prayers, provides for our needs, and loves us. As the continuing expression of the Savior's care causes us to grow in our ability to bring glory to God, so a Christian husband continues to act in ways that help his spouse to grow. His spiritual growth is reflected in his growing refusal to vacillate in his efforts to understand and care for her. The growth of each spouse requires that both husband and wife seek to nurture maturity in the other.

In the classic book *To Understand Each Other,* Paul Tournier writes of the rift that can develop in a home because the husband will not allow his wife to grow with him. Men accustomed to traditional home roles may presume that the concerns of a wife are mundane, simplistic, and without real consequence. She is concerned about Johnny's new tooth, the neighbors' latest fight, the new noise in the washer—or, of all things, uncooperative hair. Men consumed with workplace success may fail to see the importance of their wives' concerns for the security and well-being of the family reflected in these issues. Even if the wife is pursuing her own career, the husband may discover that while he discusses his job in terms of goals and tasks, she, on the other hand, speaks of her work from the perspective of personalities and tensions (or vice versa).[3]

Because they are speaking on different planes (e.g., one communicating information, the other feelings), the husband can assume his wife is incapable of understanding his concerns. As a result, he begins to withhold information from her, denying his wife aspects of himself. Eventually he finds other people with whom to share his ideas, his troubles, and even his dreams. Slowly but inevitably the man cuts his wife out of his life. Later he will complain of his boredom with her. But it is a boredom for which he is responsible. He denied her the opportunity to grow with him because he had not the patience, the courage, or the compassion to broaden either her horizons with his life or his vision with her insights.

A generation has passed since Tournier wrote. In that time the experiences of women inside and outside the home have changed dramatically, and his examples surely sound dated. However, the current popularity of gender research and books on how the sexes may relate to similar aspects of life quite differently caution us against disregarding Tournier. We may still be tempted to shut our spouses out of our deepest reflections because they do not process issues as we do. Our presumption should be that the companions God gave to complete us have valuable contributions to make to our own growth so long as we do not stifle that contribution or isolate ourselves from it.

As two vines growing together become doubly strong, protecting and benefiting each other by their respective strengths, so God intends the marriage relationship to support the development of each spouse. New gains in one support more growth in the other, enabling each to reach greater heights of spiritual maturity, character expansion, and godly honor. The biblical responsibilities of the head of a home require him to cherish and foster this growth that benefits each person and honors God. This purpose will be thwarted, however, if either person in the marriage ceases to grow—or is not allowed to grow.

When Kathy and I were first married, I was more concerned for my control of our marriage than I was for her growth. I was not trying to be cruel but was simply attempting to fulfill my biblical responsibilities as I understood them. I thought being the head of a home meant that I had to make all the decisions in our family—no matter how small. I had to decide what we would eat, whom to visit, what Kathy should wear, when we would sleep, when to get up, what cereal to buy—it was exhausting. I was drowning in decisions. In taking over the life and thought of two persons, I was struggling to keep my own head above water. I did not understand that my wife could not support me the way God designed if I gave her no opportunity to express herself. Thankfully, the Lord had my rescue and correction planned.

To comfort a friend who had recently experienced a divorce, I spent a day in his home. Despite the recentness of his separation from his wife, he had enough perspective to identify one of his major contributions to his marriage's failure. He said, "Bryan, not allowing my wife to grow was the unhealthiest thing I did to our marriage. It ruined us."

This was not a grossly evil man. He was intelligent, honest, and morally faithful to his wife. Still, the constrictive nature of his nurture would not let his wife grow. When she could stand to be stifled no more, she grew without him—and away from him.

As my friend described his dealings with his former wife, I recognized much of myself reflected in him. I listened and tried to learn what God was teaching me about the kind of leadership that fosters growth in others. Even when a man understands that the Bible requires him to encourage growth in his wife, he may not know how to go about it. Karen Howe offers these questions and insights from a woman's perspective:

> [Y]our wife has dreams and projects, too. Can you genuinely take an interest in her projects and sincerely rejoice with her when they prove successful? . . . What if she receives gifts from God's spirit that differ from your own—can you be glad for her and encourage her in their appropriate use? . . . Don't try to mold her, or suppress her; fulfill her. Honor her tastes and preferences as you honor your own, even if hers are decidedly different. . . . Paul urges Chris-

tian men to "nourish" their wives, as Christ nourishes and feeds His church. . . . This means . . . assessing her needs, physical and emotional, and trying to meet them. Could you accurately describe the areas where your wife is most in need of help?

The burden of childrearing is a heavy one, and seems to fall most heavily upon wives. If your children are not doing well in school or are having difficulties emotionally, your wife probably feels frightened and guilty. Take leadership in this, find out what the problems are, reassure her, let her know you are assuming responsibility in this area.[4]

This list of "nourishment" suggestions can be lengthened and debated. What should not elude husbands is that the nurture of their wives is a leadership responsibility. Biblical headship demands that husbands give of themselves to encourage, stimulate, and even shield the gifts and growth of their wives.

Leading by Godly Character

Since Christ gave himself for the church to cleanse her from unholiness (Eph. 5:26–27), a husband who seeks to honor Christ in his marriage will give himself for his wife's progress in overcoming sin and drawing near to God. I recognize that when I have been hurt in ministry situations, I have a tendency to recruit my wife to join in my anger. I want her to be angry along with me. I like the comfort of her assurances that I have been treated unfairly and that the problem is really the making of the other person. However, this can lead my wife into bitterness that she has difficulty shedding because she sees only how I have been hurt. I, on the other hand, have the opportunity to work through the problem with the other person. My wife does not.

After realizing that my anger can lead my wife into difficult emotions, I now try to temper the way I express to her my difficulties with others. I want to shield her from the unfairness of having to choose between supporting me and honoring God with her feelings. My headship responsibilities need to govern how I seek her sympathy as well as how I express my anger. I also must take care to remind both of us that God gives us no right to bitterness and I must be diligent in keeping Kathy informed of the status of the personal difficulty so that her heart can process the stages of resolution that I am working through. Being responsible in such expressions helps mature me even as I seek to help her.

The headship of other husbands may require similar diligence and sacrifice to shield their wives from responses that create faith challenges or temptations. A woman who is particularly prone to worry or fear or gossip or jealousy benefits from a husband who will express concerns in ways that do not engender these inappropriate reactions in her. The man who objects to his wife getting counseling help for these or more serious problems because of the embarrassment such services will cause him has tragically abandoned his headship responsibilities for selfish pride.

A basic way of helping a wife mature in her relationship with God is by taking the lead in establishing family patterns of prayer, Bible reading, and worship. Talking with a wife about her need to forgive helps bring healing for past hurts, especially if the husband acts forgiving toward her and others. Disciplining children with one's anger in control and with concern for their well-being can help everyone in the family understand that God's discipline does not deny his love. When a man appreciates the sensitivities of his wife in building family memories, in child rearing, in love-making, in home decorating, and so on, he communicates to her that he values the perspectives that God has given her. When a husband believes (and says) his wife's tenderness adds welcome dimensions to his life—rather than constraining his manhood—she will be able to believe that God made her specially to strengthen her family's bonds of love.

None of these practices, however, are more important than the pattern of godliness the husband sets in the home by his own conduct. The heart of a wife longs for the companionship and oneness with her husband that the Bible extols (see Eph. 5:31; Gen. 2:24–25; Song of Sol. 2:3–13). Thus if a man's heart wanders from God, his wife's longings to be close to her husband make his waywardness a threat to her own holiness. This is because the man tends to set the spiritual tone of the family. Wives who are spiritually mature (and personally undamaged) despite the godlessness of their husbands are rare. Despite the classic stories, it is unusual for a woman to experience healthy growth in the many dimensions of true godliness when she is married to a man disinterested in or even antagonistic to God.

Since the fundamental responsibility of all people is to grow in their ability to honor God,[5] the head of a household should encourage those in his care to learn to glorify God. Then Christ's nature will characterize the home—beginning with its leader. In our society men often relegate faith concerns to their wives. Spirituality is thought to be effeminate. However, the man who recognizes the influence of his devotion on the spiritual health of his wife and family refuses to feminize a family's faith.

The example the husband sets has eternal consequences. This means headship is more a function of controlling one's character than controlling one's wife. The man who is more concerned with how his wife should obey him than with how he should obey God fails the kindergarten of biblical headship.

Despite the wrong that should be obvious, many families remain plagued by men who defend their self-serving bullying by mouthing a few Bible verses about women needing to submit. Such husbands not only ignore specific texts requiring caring male conduct (e.g., Col. 3:19; 1 Peter 3:7) but also take out of context the Scriptures that detail God's home design. In our marriages, as well as in the world, we all remain "Christ's ambassadors, as though God were making his appeal through us" (2 Cor. 5:20).

To represent Jesus we must be willing to reflect his manner, suffer for his name, stand for his principles, and support his people—even if the place for doing so is in our families. Jesus nowhere says, Follow my example of selfless love and sacrificial care except when you are home.

With great wisdom the Bible mandates no particular style, manner, or set of behaviors that alone qualify as biblical headship. In fact there are probably as many legitimate expressions of headship as there are variations of personality. Biblical headship is simply the exercise of a God-given authority whereby a man does all that is within his power to see that love, justice, and mercy rule in his home, even where fostering such qualities requires his own personal sacrifice.[6]

In the rural town where I pastored for a number of years, a new Wal-Mart not only became the hub of retailing, it also became the social center of town. By hosting events for senior citizens as well as children, the store made itself "the place to be" for more than just the products it sold. Florence, an older woman in our church, practically made the store her second home. Shopping for "a few things I need" became a daily excuse to meet friends along the aisles, take grandchildren on shopping outings, or just share enough conversation with acquaintances to get up-to-date on the latest town happenings.

Florence's husband, Bill, was a retired carpenter who loved the outdoors. He enjoyed time at their nearby lake house, fishing and puttering. Each of them spent their days doing what they loved, though their love for each other was their deepest delight. That deep love showed itself when Florence's age no longer allowed her to drive herself to Wal-Mart. Now isolated from friends and family, she grieved when her daily excursions came to an end. But the grief did not last long.

Bill did not really understand his wife's enjoyment of Wal-Mart shopping nor did he desire to join her in it, but he soon recognized how much she missed it. One day he decided to forgo his time at the lake house. He drove Florence to Wal-Mart and stayed with her until she was ready to leave—which was not soon. On the many subsequent days that Bill took Florence to the store, he also took along a folding lawn chair. They would amble down the aisles together until Florence would strike up a conversation with a friend or stranger. Then Bill would unfold the chair and sit in the aisle until Florence was ready to proceed to the next conversation.

As he sat in the aisle, silently beaming at the enjoyment of his wife, Bill became the darling of our community. All knew his outdoor enjoyments. All knew, too, the quality of the man revealed in his sacrifice of his pleasures for hers. As a church leader in our community, Bill had taught many about the love of Jesus. His care for souls knew no societal boundaries. He was a friend to the destitute. Rebellious teens knew his care even when their parents had given up on them. Bill refused to recognize racial lines long before civil rights laws required the community to address its prejudices. Bill's leadership was beyond dispute, because his character was beyond reproof. By giving himself for his wife in their later years, Bill was simply heading his family as he had led his life. His lawn chair was a symbol of the sacrifice that made his leadership so effective and noble.

Christ's Sacrifice

How can husbands live so? How can men sacrifice so? By recognizing that the ultimate resource God provides for Christian husbanding is Christ's sacrifice. It may seem disingenuous that Paul—so obviously speaking of the man/woman relationship in this key biblical passage that details standards for Christian marriage—says, "This is a profound mystery—but I am talking about Christ and the church" (Eph. 5:32). I am tempted to accuse Paul of joking here. "C'mon, Paul," I instinctively respond, "you know you are really talking more about earthly than spiritual relationships." Yet the more I look into my own heart, the more I see that the apostle must mean his words. A husband's biblical love for his wife finds its root and resources in his knowledge of Christ's love.

Because Christ gave himself for our sin, we can know God's approval even if we have failed to live up to his or our expectations. Christ's sacrifice on our behalf fulfills God's requirements, allowing us to have an eternal relationship with him. Those who trust in Jesus' provision are assured of the acceptance and approval of the King of the universe, regardless of their achievements or standing in the world. In God's eyes we are robed in the righteousness of his own Son, and thus the heavenly honor and love due Christ is ours to claim as well. When a man is secure in this knowledge, he does not need to live at the expense of his spouse, seeking affirmation of his worth by the esteem or service he can demand of her.

If a husband is not secure in his relationship with his Savior— if a man needs to have control over another to have some confidence in himself—then he cannot love as God requires. Christ's love is our relational fuel. If our spiritual lives are running on empty, then we will inevitably suck energy from the life of our marriages. Men who assert or confirm their manhood by the psychological, physical, or sexual control of their spouses actually reveal deep insecurities of the soul that leech personal esteem from the misery of others. Until the certainty of God's approval fills the wells of need in a man's heart, he will always be tempted to drain life from others, including those nearest and dearest to him.

Recently I was summoned to another town to try to help restore the relationship of an estranged couple. On the way from the airport the husband told me how much he loved his wife and how desperate he was for her to return home. Later that evening his wife picked us up in the family car to drive to a restaurant where we could begin our discussions. The planned conversations never occurred.

On the way to dinner the husband could not restrain his comments about the wife's driving habits, the shoddy maintenance she was giving the car, the way she had allowed their children to play with the radio controls, and the route she had chosen to take to the restaurant. By the time we arrived at our dining place, the husband had his wife so flustered and unsure of herself that she was too nervous to eat.

From the backseat I watched as the man, who hours before had told me how much he loved his wife, now tried to control her by magnifying her self-doubt and manipulating her emotional stress. This was not love; it was a cruel attempt to control another for the man's own purposes. He was so desperate for his wife's return that he was willing to destroy her self-confidence to make her dependent on him.

The man's friends, family, and boss had urged him to try to mend the broken marriage. It became more and more apparent that in large measure he was seeking reconciliation because he needed their approval rather than because of mature concern for his wife. My pastoral task over the next two days was to help the man understand that God's grace held him so surely that he could find release from the insecurities that made him need his wife's dependence. Then he could free his wife to love him rather than to need him. Further, he could lead his wife to find her own security in the Savior.

We will have no ability to serve each other as God requires if we are not sure of our standing in Christ. Through confidence in their eternal standing men find the courage to make earthly decisions that require sacrifice for the good of others. Christ alone provides this personal security men require to head their homes as God desires. When a man no longer questions his ultimate worth, he can rightly weigh his family's good against accepting a promotional transfer, a prestigious community office, or even the need to win an argument with his wife.

Great Christian leadership always flows from meditation on the Savior's great love. Six years after resigning his high-profile position to care for his wife, Robertson McQuilkin wrote of what had maintained him through the drain and pain of caring for his stricken wife:

> "How do you do it? What are your resources?" asked the host on the television show *Day of Discovery.* I hadn't thought about it, but since then I have. Praise helps. Right now, I think my life must be happier than 95 percent of the people on planet earth. Muriel's a joy to me, and life is good to both of us, in different ways. But I'm thinking of something more basic than "counting your blessings."
>
> By 1992, the blows of life had left me numb—my dearest slipping from me, my eldest son snatched away in a tragic accident, my life's work abandoned at its peak. I didn't hold it against God, but my faith could better be described as resignation. The joy had drained away, the passion in my love for God had frozen over. I was in trouble. . . .
>
> Of course, the passion of his [Christ's] love for me had never cooled. Even in my darkest hours when I felt my grip slipping and was in danger of sliding into the abyss of doubt, what always caught and held me was the vision of God's best loved, pinioned in my place. . . .
>
> Then I remembered the secret I had learned in younger days—going to a mountain hideaway to be alone with God. There, though it was slow in coming, I was able to break free from preoccupation with my troubles and concentrate on Jesus. When that happened, I relearned what God had taught me more than once before: the heavy heart lifts on wings of praise.[7]

Praising God for the "pinioned" Savior renewed this wonderful leader's heart and headship commitments. The grace that provides pardon beyond our achievements also provides strength beyond our abilities.

Only when our hearts are sure of God's unmerited favor—his grace—do we have the means we need to maintain a Christian marriage. Without a solid relationship with our Lord, we simply do not have the personal security necessary to sacrifice for the good of another. The ultimate resource we have that enables us to love as Christ requires is Christ's love for us. That is why, when he gives marriage instructions, Paul even more carefully spells out the assurance we have of God's love for us through the sacrifice of his Son. When we rest in his love, we can reflect it. The degree of confidence we have in the strength of his care for us will largely determine the measure of selfless tenderness we can express.

Husbands—and wives—I know I have not in these few pages answered all of your questions about how Christian headship should be expressed in marriage. Most of us have much to learn about this biblical imperative, but the path to our understanding and obedience remains graciously plain. If a husband's constant effort, consistent motivation, and deep desire is to love as he is confident Jesus loves him, then that man's leadership choices are neither as obscure nor as harsh as the world tempts us to imagine.

When Robertson McQuilkin first wrote of his decision to resign his position at one of the nation's prestigious evangelical institutions to care for his wife, he reported that he was startled by the response he received. Husbands and wives who heard the account renewed their marriage vows; pastors told the story to their congregations; young people attested to a rekindled desire for a marriage commitment their culture had previously taught them to minimize and devalue.

McQuilkin said, "It was a mystery to me [why so many were responding so passionately to his care for his wife] until a distinguished oncologist, who lives constantly with dying people, told me, 'Almost all women stand by their men; very few men stand by their women.'"[8]

How curious that in dying to self and becoming a servant to his wife, this man became a leader of men and women across this nation. There is really no mystery in this. McQuilkin's actions merely reflect the heart of the gospel. They are a mirror of Christ's ministry that should enlighten all our marriages: We lead most clearly, most effectively, most authoritatively, and most like Christ when we live most sacrificially.

One husband became a leader to many when in active obedience to Christ he applied his gifts, talents, authority, and calling to the nurture and care of a loved one. God calls us to believe that, in a similar way, each man becomes a leader in his family when he exercises his gifts, abilities, and rights in the service of his loved ones. The Lord who submitted himself to the cross on our behalf calls husbands to be no less submissive to his will by being servant/leaders in their homes. There the biblical heads of households take the lead in dying to self as their Christian mission and marital joy, to Christ's glory. The path to Christian leadership in the home is always the way of the cross.

Part 2

The Sacrificial Wife
Noble Love

Wives, submit to your husbands as to the Lord. For the husband is the head of the wife as Christ is the head of the church, his body, of which he is the Savior. Now as the church submits to Christ, so also wives should submit to their husbands in everything.

Ephesians 5:22–24

I was in my first days as a seminary professor. He was in his last days as a seminary president. Still, though his days at the school and on this earth were nearing their completion, Dr. Robert G. Rayburn, the founding president of Covenant Theological Seminary, had invited my wife and me to his home for dinner. Though it was his custom to welcome new professors in this way, the cancer Dr. Rayburn was fighting made this invitation particularly meaningful to us—and difficult for him.

Seated at the head of the table, President Rayburn remained the unquestioned authority figure in the house despite the weakening of his body. His bearing and manner remained almost regal, though his hands quivered a bit when he served each of us our meal. His habit through the years at such dinners was to serve his guests and his wife from a side table before taking his own food. Now the cancer had made the movements of this service painful and awkward. The custom continued only because Mrs. Rayburn had stacked our plates on the table near Dr. Rayburn's place and had rolled a cart with serving dishes next to his chair.

He served us because she helped him do so. This was only the beginning of her service. Throughout the evening we watched in silent admiration as she preserved his dignity and enabled him to function in a manner appropriate to his position, through her deft and subtle gestures. The steadied hand, the occasionally completed sentence, the slight movement of an article of furniture that kept him from tripping enabled him to serve us and preserve his honor, while they ennobled her. The dignity she provided him became her own since only by her aid did he fulfill his purposes.

The events of that evening are forever etched in our minds as a poignant display of the home relationships the Bible promotes. The head of the home used his authority to serve others, including his wife. In turn, the wife used her gifts to support that authority, and so her efforts served both him and those he served. As each gave of self for the good of the other, each supported (even enabled) the actions of the other and shared in the other's dignity.

What does God expect women to do to promote this mutual dignity in their homes? The complexities of our age and the confusion in our culture about the family responsibilities of women require us to examine Scripture with extreme care to make sure answers to this question are not merely derived from personal opinion or present circumstances. As we consider what the Bible says, I need to be very clear about my goal. Since I challenged men to resist cultural trends and remember their biblical responsibilities in the first part of this book, readers may think that it is now my intention to impose demeaning expectations on modern women and make them feel guilty for unfulfilled duties. Nothing could be further from the truth of my or Scripture's intentions.

God's purpose for all persons in the home is that we may be dispensers of his grace to the family. When we understand how he can use us to share the message of his own unconditional love, then the means he gives us to fulfill that purpose become blessings rather than burdens. As we share ourselves the way God designs, the family is knit together and each member finds unequaled meaning, purpose, and security. In this environment love prospers, joy thrives, and the dignity of each person grows.

four

A Woman's Responsibility
The Completion of Another

When Fergie married Prince Andrew, we marveled at the days of pageantry surrounding the royal wedding, but what most remember is a moment when their vows were taken. Fergie was supposed to say to her groom, "I promise to love, honor, and *obey* . . ." She did say the phrase, but not without a sideways glance and grin at the Prince that said much more. Her look could hardly have more clearly articulated the new Duchess's thought: "You gotta be kidding. Nobody really believes those anachronisms about wifely submission anymore, and *you* had better not!"

She repeated the vows, but with a toss of her head Fergie as clearly tossed away the content of those words without any indication of what commitments should or could take their place. In hindsight, her careless lip service to traditions she did not truly intend to honor has become a sad metaphor for a royal marriage gone awry. But it is not merely royalty to whom the metaphor applies.

If we listen past the lip service that we too readily pay to the official positions of our churches, political parties, families, or traditions, we also are likely to find large question marks about the current responsibilities of women in marriage. A campus minister at Vanderbilt University said recently, "It does not matter whether the intelligent women on this campus are liberal feminists or conservative traditionalists; if you can get them to talk honestly about their deepest concerns, most will say that they constantly wonder if their personal choices are correct. Deep down they are desperate for a credible authority to help them decide what women are supposed to be."[1]

Sadly our churches have not proved to be a credible or consistent enough authority to settle the issue. Some ecclesiastical leaders have urged women fed up with abusive husbands to leave their marriages. Other churches have used discipline to try to force women to submit to husbands guilty of the same offenses under the assumption that the abuse is a result of the women not being submissive enough. I hear the resultant confusion among my own relatives as women, long committed to marriage and deeply desiring to honor Scripture, have cried out in emotional exhaustion and spiritual agony, "I know that the Bible says to submit but I can't continue to live this way. I have tried but I can't keep on. I just can't."

From palaces to campuses to churches to our homes the questions echo: How really is a wife supposed to love; how should she honor; should she obey? Flip answers that do not consider the challenges of our times, the dignity of each person, and the authority of God's Word will neither satisfy us nor glorify our God. He is too concerned for his people to leave us without principles to guide and govern our most precious relationships.

So what is a Christian wife to do? The plain answer stated in Scripture is that a Christian wife is to submit. The Bible says, "Wives, submit to your husbands as to the Lord" (Eph. 5:22).[2] However, neither mouthing ancient dogma nor mindlessly shouting, Submit, at modern women (nor even studying the original meaning of that biblical term—a combination of words meaning "to arrange under") will settle today's concerns. The true duty, dignity, and beauty God intends for wives unfolds only as we consider the significance of his intentions for them.

Submission Does *Not* Mean Nothing

God's desire for women to submit to their husbands reflects no passing or incidental concern. God considers the submission of wives extremely important. The apostle Paul reflects the degree of God's concern by describing the duty as having eternal as well as earthly consequences.

The Scope of the Apostle's Words

A Compelling Expression

Despite our culture's aversion to the notion of anybody submitting to anybody, we have trouble sidestepping Paul's broadly encompassing words about wives' submission. The importance of submission is first reflected in the compelling expression in which the duty is couched. Wives are to submit to their husbands "as to the Lord" (Eph. 5:22). This biblical phrasing does not mean that a wife should treat her husband as though he were God. We are not to make idols out of anything or anyone. Rather, the words indicate that a woman's submission is motivated not so much by a husband's deserving as by God's purposes. She renders the service the Bible requires as to God himself (with all appropriate devotion and joy), rather than simply to another human (whose failings may make her service seem unfair and onerous). The idea is that as a woman submits to her husband, she looks over his shoulder to see the Lord who is saying, "You are ultimately doing this not for him but for me."

Submission motivated by love for the Savior who suffered on the cross for us can help a woman whose friends or her own inclinations encourage her to base her submissive actions (or nonactions) on her husband's worthiness. Such false encouragers may whisper, Why should you serve the good of a person like that if he treats you so poorly or is so unappealing or has so little potential for making you happy? These voices tempt us to submit to God's purposes only when the person we serve makes it worthwhile for us to do so.

The Bible, on the contrary, encourages each of us to obey God in the way we relate to one another in the home (as well as in the workplace and in the community), not because other persons deserve our service but because God deserves our devotion. The fact that God would use us for his purposes explains the necessity for our service, provides proper motive for our obedience, and underscores the importance of it.

For more than thirty years after she committed herself to living for the Savior who died for her, the wife of a police captain in our town prayed for her husband to make the same commitment. In the early years of her marriage, she confesses, she tried to preach him into a commitment to Christ or to manipulate him into church. When he responded to none of her arguments or ploys, however, she ultimately resolved merely to love him despite his grizzled manner and occasional mocking of her faith.

For many more years she cared for her husband with the "gentle and quiet spirit" that the apostle Peter advises for the wives of husbands who are not Christians (1 Peter 3:4). Finally, the hardened police captain did respond to the witness of his wife. Now he too has confessed his need of Jesus and serves the Savior with an equally gentle and quiet heart.

Once I asked this wife, who had waited for so long for her husband's heart to change, what had kept her living sacrificially for her husband for more than three decades. Unspoken but understood between us was also the question of how she had continued to live for his good when his manner often made her life painful and hard. She responded simply, "When I became a Christian, I fell in love with Jesus. My love for him made me want to do what he wanted for my husband."

When a wife submits to her husband "as to the Lord," heaven's purposes powerfully compel her, even when human rewards seem remote. By bringing this heavenly perspective into view, the apostle makes it clear that a wife's responsibility is not removed simply because her experience with a husband is difficult. As all persons should arrange their lives under the righteous purposes of their Lord, so wives should prioritize their lives so as to serve the purposes God has for their husbands.

An Example

To clarify the nature of a wife's submission to her husband the apostle next supplies an *example* for comparison. He says that as the church submits to the headship of Christ, so wives should submit to their husbands' headship (Eph. 5:24). As the church could never fulfill its purposes without submitting to the holy will of the Lord, the apostle reminds women that they cannot fulfill God's intentions for them if they do not submit to the biblical purposes of their husbands. Obviously this example constrains the wife by requiring her to submit her will to that of her husband so that God's plans for the home will prosper. A woman disobeys God when she ignores, undermines, or counters the properly expressed authority of her husband. At the same time, the apostle's example frees the wife from submission to ungodly demands since the church's submission to Christ never includes participation in evil or yielding to what dishonors God's plan for his people.

Through the ages, the church has often erred by teaching women that they must do whatever a husband wants regardless of its moral or personal consequences. Because a wife is to submit to her husband as the church submits to Christ, a woman is always morally and spiritually responsible for her own actions. A husband has no right to require of his wife what is contrary to God, and she has no obligation to obey what forces her, him, or their family from God's will. The requirement to submit to one's husband never takes precedence over the requirement to submit to God. Submission is an act of worship whose primary purpose is to honor God. This means that a woman remains responsible for exercising spiritual discretion and strength in order to support her husband in ways that promote godliness in the home. The home will not function as God intends if the wife does not continue to mature in her own spiritual understanding so that she possesses the spiritual strength her husband's support requires.

The Comprehensive Extent

Finally, lest we assume Paul only means these standards to apply to some narrow part of life, the apostle clarifies the *comprehensive extent* of his instruction by saying that "wives should submit to their husbands *in everything*" (Eph. 5:24, italics mine). As already noted, these words do not mean that women should submit to evil demands or incompetent authority. If the goal of submission is to honor God, then wives cannot yield to what he would not approve. However, the apostle makes it clear that a wife should not submit to her husband only in church or only regarding a certain category of decisions or only when the submission is easy and agreeable. The Bible requires a wife to respect the authority God gives her husband in every dimension of their relationship (vv. 24, 33).

In this age when the careers of a husband and wife may conflict, when dramatically different views about child rearing or money management divide couples, and when much of our culture says no one's will should have priority over another's, it may be extremely difficult for a woman to submit to the authority of her husband. The Bible does not belittle this difficulty, but neither does it annul a husband's authority. Should our minds object that the Bible's writers simply did not anticipate the nature of modern society, we should remember that God gave these instructions when the sophisticates of Greek and Roman society were also blurring any distinctions in the home responsibilities of men and women.

When the home is functioning biblically, the husband will consult and honor his wife's input into family decisions and actions. Caring compromise whenever possible characterizes the home where husband and wife are seeking to honor God and each other as the Bible directs. The Bible tells husbands to be considerate of their wives and to treat them with *respect*—the same word used to describe how we are to honor kings.[3] However, even when this regard is not given, the Bible reminds wives to respect their husbands' decisions so long as they do not demand disobedience to God.

When a wife loses respect for her husband, the marriage can quickly weaken. Early in our marriage Kathy enjoyed spending part of summer evenings at a neighbor's home where her friends gathered around a porch swing. The evenings were full of laughter and teasing, but after a few weeks Kathy stopped joining the others. Though she loved the time with her friends, she said that their humor increasingly came at the expense of their husbands. The wives seemed to delight in exchanging tales of the stupidities and eccentricities of their mates. Kathy said she felt increasingly out of place (even though her husband's faults and foibles could have provided her a rich supply of anecdotes) because she did not feel she could honor Scripture and participate in the ridicule. Kathy said, "I can't make fun of you in someone else's home, and respect you in our home."

My wife's honest expression of how difficult it is to maintain true respect for a spouse in one arena of life when it does not exist in another helps explain why the apostle's words are so encompassing. Scripture says there should be no aspect of life and no time of life when a woman fails to submit to the biblical authority of her husband. That really is *comprehensive*.

The Scope of Scripture's Witness

Though the apostle Paul's marriage instruction is comprehensive, still we could choose to narrow or disregard his words if they seemed to be an exception to what Scripture teaches elsewhere. If we could show that these words about a wife's submission were merely an isolated reference in an obscure verse, then our culture as well as sound Bible interpretation principles would require us to downplay what seems so sure to offend so many. We might correctly conclude that the command for wives to submit does not really mean anything for today if these words in Ephesians are unique in Scripture. The validity of such a conclusion fades, however, in light of Scripture's consistent and repeated support of the submission concept.

The requirement for wives to submit to their husbands is not limited to one obscure verse. At least three separate times in the

Ephesians passage, Paul instructs wives to subject themselves to their husbands' authority (Eph. 5:22–24, 33). The apostle actually uses this same or related terminology to teach about wives submitting to their husbands in five of his epistles—1 Corinthians, Ephesians, Colossians, 1 Timothy, and Titus. Such teaching is not Paul's alone. The apostle Peter also tells wives, "be submissive to your husbands so that, if any of them do not believe the word, they may be won over without words by the behavior of their wives" (1 Peter 3:1).

The New Testament writers take pains to assure readers that their requirements for women are neither novel nor unique to their age. Peter commends the submission of wives to the authority of their husbands in his era because "the holy women of the past who put their hope in God . . . were submissive to their own husbands" (v. 5). How far into the past this standard applied is also reflected in the biblical analogies Peter uses to back his instruction. Peter ties the submissive spirit, which he requires of wives, to Israel's earliest history. He encourages wives to be "like Sarah" who two thousand years previously had "obeyed Abraham and called him her master" (v. 6). Paul goes back even farther in the Ephesians and Corinthians passages by relating his instruction to the order of husband/wife relationships established at creation (Eph. 5:31; 1 Cor. 11:7–10).

Scripture's instruction for wives to submit to their husbands is remarkably sweeping and consistent. Far from being limited to an obscure reference, the concept appears across Paul's letters, reappears in other New Testament writing, finds precedent in Israel's origins, and has its design conceived at humanity's creation. Godly instruction so comprehensive in scope cannot mean nothing for Christians concerned to honor their Lord with their lives.

Submission Does Mean Something

The significance Scripture gives to the teaching about wives submitting to their husbands should prevent us from discounting the message. We cannot sweep aside as inconsequential or without meaning what receives such frequent attention from those who wrote under God's inspiration. Still, knowing that the submission concept is important does not tell us all we need to know. We still have to know what submission means. The original word is a combination of Greek terms that in very rough translation would mean something like, "to arrange under."[4] In common usage submission conveyed ideas of obedience and subservience.

From the precise biblical contexts in which the term is used, commentators variously interpret submission as "a disposition to yield," "voluntary yielding in love," or "not to exercise authority over."[5] To these technical ideas can be added the colloquial commentary that biblical submission means that "a wife should follow her husband's lead, but it does not mean that she should be her husband's shadow."[6] Though the specific definitions vary a little, it is apparent that submission includes actions, since it involves *obedience* (1 Peter 3:5–6),[7] and it includes attitudes, since it involves *respect* (Eph. 5:33). These word studies help, but we do not really know what God expects of wives until we see the context in which the apostles use the term *submit.*

To Complete Another

What biblical submission means is perhaps most obvious in light of the purposes it fulfills. Paul begins to disclose these purposes when he refers to the genesis of the marriage relationship, saying, "'For this reason a man will leave his father and mother and be united to his wife, and the two will become one flesh.' This is a profound mystery . . ." (Eph. 5:31–32). These words remind us that marriage commits two people to a union that forms their mutual completeness, even as they give of themselves to provide for the good of each other. A marriage will never fulfill God's purposes for the couple or for the individual partners if either abandons care for the fulfillment of the other. Thus one dimension of a wife's responsibility involves *the pouring of herself into the completion of her husband.*

Sacrificing one's self to make a relationship (and those in it) whole defines the essence of biblical submission. Still, the subtleties and complexities of any marriage defy attempts to simplify submission to a few rules for home etiquette. Paul says the ways in which two become one is "a profound mystery," and we can well attest to that. It is so past our explaining (and yet so obvious to us) that God has made those of us who are not gifted for celibacy[8] never quite whole—in our relational maturity, our personal development, and even our spirituality—without the one who will complement and complete us in marital oneness.

The connection of personal wholeness to marital completion becomes evident as we look at another individual (or even at ourselves) after a few years of marriage and observe: That person has so matured, so leveled out, or become so much less self-absorbed since marrying so and so. At least that is what we say if the marriage is functioning well. If the marriage is going poorly, we typically recognize that the individual's self-absorption, immaturity, or character flaws are even more prominent.

If you are dishonest with your spouse, the one God intends for you to know most intimately, you will necessarily give up aspects of spiritual development that are needed to safeguard your integrity in other areas of life. A person engaged in an extramarital affair not only damages the oneness of the marriage but stunts his or her own character development. Lack of consideration for one's spouse (in habits, conversation, or faithfulness) almost always creates an individual whom others see as self-centered and ruthless. Seeking their own advantage, neighbors and coworkers may laugh at the jokes and cater to the interests of such an individual but they know better than to trust a person who does not honor the trust of marriage.

When the real oneness that God intends for marriage does not occur, then the persons in that relationship become less than whole. Though this is a mystery, it fits precisely with Scripture, which tells us that since God's purpose for marriage is to make each spouse whole, the abuse or neglect of that union must damage both persons (see Gen. 2:20–24; Eph. 5:31).

This knowledge of the ways in which our lives affect each other helps shape our understanding of what the apostle says here about the mutual responsibilities of marriage. To the husband Scripture gives the authority for the sacrificial responsibility of biblical headship that is designed to lead a family in the paths of God. To the wife, God commits the nurture and supportive care of the husband so that he can carry out these duties. At creation God made the woman to help the man fulfill his responsibilities. She was to be his "helper"—"a help meet (i.e., suitable or compatible) for him" say the historic translations (Gen. 2:18; 1 Cor. 11:8–9). Far from being a demeaning term, the "helper" term refers to God himself or his actions elsewhere in Scripture.[9] Thus the helper language reminds us that a wife fulfills heavenly purposes in her home.

God intends for each wife to complement her husband so that together they fulfill God's expectations for their lives more completely than either could separately. Each has responsibility for the other to the end that the family unit is whole and healthy before God. Elisabeth Elliot captures this purpose well:

> The first woman was made specifically for the first man, a helper, to meet, respond to, surrender to, and complement him. God made her *from* the man, out of his very bone, and then he brought her *to* the man. When Adam named Eve, he accepted responsibility to "husband" her—to provide for her, to cherish her, to protect her. These two people together represent the image of God—one of them in a special way the initiator, the other the responder. Neither the one nor the other was adequate alone to bear the divine image.[10]

The wife's complementary gifts help complete the spiritual character of her husband, even as God uses the man's maturing character to lead all members of the family (including the wife) in paths that honor Christ. In this way the wife fulfills a redemptive purpose in the home, enabling each person more fully to know and be what the Savior desires by submitting herself in love to the good of another.

A wife who offered herself for the completion of her home and husband surfaced in the confession of a friend who visited my family. My friend, whom I will only identify here as Steve, came to see us when he and his family were in trouble—because of him.

87

When Steve was a child, his father intentionally drove Steve's psychologically fragile mother into insanity in order to have an uninterrupted affair with a neighbor. So horrible was Steve's childhood that he said he could not remember a single conversation with a parent, nor did he ever see a healthy interchange between his mother and father.

The trauma of his childhood was now reaching into the family of his adulthood. Because of the absence of healthy family memories or models in his childhood, Steve now confessed he did not know how to relate to his own wife and children. That is why he came to observe our family. He said, "I must have new family memories to draw on so that I can love my family as I should."

What Steve did not tell us at the beginning of his visit was the event that had caused him to seek our help. That very painful revelation came later.

Despite deeply loving his family, Steve had little control over a violent temper. A little more than a year prior to his visit, a particularly angry rage had scared even Steve. When he had calmed down, he promised his wife that if he ever lost his temper like that again he would leave her and the children for their own protection. Steve said that he did not want to subject his own family to the kind of endless trauma in which he had been raised.

In the year following his promise, little changed in Steve's behavior. The angry episodes continued unabated.

Steve's wife never responded in kind to his rages and she never reminded him of his promise. She endured his anger without reaction for a year. On the anniversary of Steve's promise, he launched into another rage. This time his wife ran to the bedroom and began to weep uncontrollably.

His wife's unprecedented response and obvious grief sobered Steve. He sat on the bed beside her and asked, "Honey, what is it? You never let my fits upset you like this before." Then she reminded him of the promise.

"A year ago on this date," she said, "you told me that you would leave me and the children if you continued to lose your temper. When you made that promise, I knew that you could not control your anger. I didn't know what to do. So, I went to our pastor. I told him what you had said and I asked what I should do. I didn't want to lose you. I don't want you to leave."

She continued, "The pastor told me that I could not change you—only God can do that—but that I could pray for you. So every day I have prayed for you. I have asked God to take away your temper and I have never reminded you of what you said. But you haven't changed. When you lost your temper today, a year after you made that horrible promise, I started to lose hope. I love you so much, but I don't know what to do anymore."

What she had already done is what changed Steve. Daily she had given herself for him in faithful prayer and care without resentment. When he realized how long his wife had applied every ounce of her spiritual resources to helping him and holding their family together, his heart and pride broke. That is when he came to our family seeking help because he wanted so much to respond to the sacrifice of his wife.

The changes in Steve were not immediate, but they were definite and progressive. He matured into the kind of husband and father God desired him to be as a result of the support God designed and enabled his wife to give. God used her "gentle and quiet spirit" (1 Peter 3:4) to give Steve the resolve and strength he needed to heal the wounds of his past and to lead his family into a unified future. He and his family are now more spiritually, relationally, and emotionally whole because his wife poured her heart into the completion of her husband.

The specific actions to which God calls other wives may be quite different as they consider how they contribute to the completion of their husbands. Some may be called to greater sacrifice. Others may find that God will use a favorite activity or special talent to encourage a husband, or simply teach him how to have fun. God did not make marriages with a cookie cutter, and the ways in which wives may support, complement, and complete their spouses are usually open to a lifetime of discovery.

Perhaps nothing is more key in the process, however, than remembering that the goal is helping a spouse be what God intends. A wife who is devoted to making a husband what *she* intends indicates that she does not love her husband for what he is but for what she wants to make him. A wife who marries with the intention of reforming her husband rarely loves him deeply. Instead, she delays giving her whole heart to him until after he reflects the perfection of her makeover. Thus she is forever deprived of oneness with her spouse as he is in the present. A reforming wife dedicates herself to making a man in her image; a biblical wife gives herself to God, allowing him to use her in developing his image in her husband.

To Honor Another

Scripture consistently articulates what attitudes are required for a woman to support her spouse, but the actions required are never as completely described. God tells us to sacrifice for each other but he does not provide a universal grid of activities or habits into which every couple must fit their lives. The Bible nowhere says who should take out the garbage or carry in groceries from the car. There is a remarkable absence of such prescriptions in Scripture for the daily operations of a marriage. Apparently the goal of wholeness and health for the family is far more important than any specific set of behaviors that all couples should observe despite differing personalities, gifts, and circumstances. This means that, while it is impossible not to be influenced by stereotypical behaviors in our culture, merely confining women to the roles a society determines to be wifely will not fulfill the Bible's mandates for wives.

The inappropriateness of limiting a wife's responsibilities to cultural expectations becomes obvious when we understand that submission (in addition to requiring the pouring of oneself into the completion of another) involves *the exercising of gifts for the glory of another.* This purpose becomes most apparent in the light of the balanced construction of Paul's words to wives *and* husbands. The apostle directs husbands to use their headship as Christ did for the glory of his bride, the church (Eph. 5:25–27). A husband must never abuse his authority so that he robs his wife of "radiance" (v. 27). At the same time a wife is to submit so as not to rob her husband of "respect" (v. 33).

Discerning how wives should fulfill their obligation to honor their husbands requires us to unroll the implications of Paul's comparison of marriage to the relationship of Christ and the church. The church does not honor Christ by dispensing with the gifts and graces God provides. Rather, God calls her to arrange all her energies and abilities under the grand purpose of glorifying the Savior. To do less would not be submission; it would be disobedience. For instance, the gifts of music God gives the church are not to be suppressed, but used fully for praising him. To suppress the church's music would be to deny God his due glory. Such gifts must find their proper avenues, of course, but simply to mute or dismantle the gifts would deny the wisdom of the God who gave them and requires their proper use.

By following this line of thought, we gather the wisdom of Paul's terminology. Biblical submission truly is an "arranging under" of one's own resources and abilities for the glory of another.[11] Such submission is never an abdication of responsibility for another's welfare, nor is it an abandonment of one's own gifts to fit a predetermined behavior mold. Biblical submission requires a woman always to explore how to use the unique gifts and abilities God has given her to make the glory of God's image most evident in her spouse and home.

Each wife must determine how she can best bring the glory of God into her marriage. Universal directives based on societal preferences are inappropriate. The Bible does not specify who drives the car, who writes checks for the monthly bills, or how many hours outside of the home a spouse may work or play without crossing some definite threshold of marital correctness. In fact the ideal wife of Proverbs 31 engages in a great range of domestic, charitable, and business activities. However, the Bible commends such a woman, not because of her industry alone but because of the support and respect she brings her husband through her endeavors (see Prov. 31:11–12, 23, 28).

Neither accepting nor rejecting cultural norms will guarantee that biblical priorities are honored. The responsibilities of marriage are only determined at the deepest levels of the heart and call for diligent, honest, and conscientious self-examination. The husband must ask not only, *Am I leading my family to a better knowl-*

91

edge of God? but also, *Is my leadership self-serving or sacrificial?* The wife must similarly ask not only, *Do my actions, words, and attitudes support my husband so as to enable him to lead my family to a better knowledge of God?* but also, *Have I truly in everything submitted my life to this highest priority?* These are questions that cannot be answered by arbitrary, traditional, or merely habitual role assignments.

When a woman, or her spouse, determines that she will not use her gifts for the good of the family, then the glory that God intends for both husband and wife is damaged. This truth is sadly evident in the marriage of distant friends of ours. The husband is a church leader who sits on a council that examines new pastoral candidates. Of every new candidate he asks the same question: "Does your wife submit to you?" The man wants each potential pastor to prove to the council that he has control of his family the way the official thinks headship should be practiced—meaning the way he controls his own family. However, it would be tragic if candidates actually did answer the way that this official desires.

Over the years this man's friends have watched as his intelligent, once glowing and buoyant wife has become increasingly silent, sullen, and dowdy under his "headship." The more withdrawn she has become, the more obnoxious, belligerent, and accusing he has become with everyone in his path. The more she retreats from her own gifts, the more his excesses assert themselves.

This wife is not to blame for her husband's faults, but his friends cannot help but see in him the consequences of the suppression of his spouse's gifts. Still, despite the obvious deterioration of their family's witness, both parties in this marriage claim the wife is biblically submitting to her husband because she talks only when he allows, leaves the home only when he permits, and wears only what he approves. How sad! By limiting headship and submission to a certain set of preconceived behaviors, both individuals have actually lost sight of their true biblical priorities of promoting God's glory in each other. Thus they have diminished each other.

I cannot prescribe the specific actions this wife should take each day, nor do I pretend to know precisely what should have changed between these two people years ago. We should recognize, however, that submitting one's life to the good of another does not mean abandoning that person to his or her faults nor abandoning one's own gifts.

To Mature Another

As we have seen, submission to a spouse should never be interpreted as requiring a wife to sin because her husband demands it. In a similar way, a woman should not betray the reasons God placed her in the marriage by submitting to misguided authority. If a husband is abusing his authority or abandoning his spiritual obligations, then the duty of a wife committed to her husband's good is "no longer conscientiously to submit, but conscientiously to refuse to do so."[12] She must use the heart and brains God gave her along with the humility and courage he requires to promote the glory God intends for her husband. Writes Kent Hughes:

> The fact that a wife wants to honor her husband's leadership if possible does not mean she will sit in mute silence. Questioning his reasoning or acquainting him with his error is not evidence of a rebellious spirit, but rather of love. Refusing to support his moral folly is not sin. A Christian wife can stand with Christ against her husband with a humble, loving spirit which indicates her longing to honor his headship. The attitude is, of course, key.[13]

A woman married to a difficult man, of course, must make such decisions with great care, and usually with great patience (Note: The godly counsel of the church is also indispensable in serious matters). I do not want to understate the pain that also may be involved in discerning how best to apply these biblical principles in a difficult marriage, nor the importance of applying them in a good marriage. To apply them effectively and correctly, a wife must understand the gifts God has given her and how her husband and her marriage benefit when she uses them.[14] *Biblical submission ultimately is not the suppression of gifts but the full expression of them on behalf of another.*

Each of us brings to the marriage a unique personality, set of talents, and background that God intends to use to make our homes (and each person in them) better reflect the love and character of his Son. God does not want anyone to trash these gifts. By the use and interaction of each partner's unique talents, God intends to mature each person according to a divine strategy that began functioning when he made these two persons one. This design reflects the wisdom and craft of God's own creative character. However, we deny ourselves and each other the beauty of this design when we bottle up the gifts he wants our lives to express.

Of course there may be ways that each person in the marriage must temporarily set aside or more permanently direct his or her gifts for the marriage to function well. A spouse with a gift for socializing may need to curb the desire to respond to every party invitation out of respect for the feelings of a mate who is naturally shy. However, the spouse who is more sociable may also use his or her gift to teach the partner how to enjoy such occasions and deepen other relationships. My wife has provided this specific service to me, and as a result, I am able to meet the expectations of my job in a way I could never have done without her influence.

Much more difficult compromises may need to be made when balancing careers, making moving plans, or deciding how best to care for children. I do not want to minimize the difficulty of such decisions. Still, such decisions are made less torturous when both spouses realize that neither has a right to disregard the gifts of the other and that various compromises may be God's way of promoting the glory he intends for each spouse.

Limiting the definition of biblical submission to a specific set of traditionally prescribed chores or conventions is a result of faulty thinking that creates sadness and oppression in marriage. In the context of their culture, marriage, situation, personal interests, and individual gifts, each couple must determine how each person will fulfill his or her marriage responsibilities. Not to use their gifts would betray both the reason God gave the gifts and the requirement that they be used for another's good. This does not mean that a woman's gifts should determine what she does. Rather, what God calls her to do (in supporting her husband and home) should determine how she uses her gifts. God gives us gifts to help us fulfill our responsibilities, not to alter his designs for our relationships.

By the qualities they bring to the marriage, some wives teach their husbands tenderness. Many add to their husbands' strength. Each wife should discover the pleasure of using the unique ways God has enabled her to make her husband know he is special in her eyes, for as she does so, the man knows the deepest pleasures of God's care even when other aspects of life are troubling. The woman who submits her life to God's purposes enables a man to know the glory of being treasured by God, even when the world seems to disregard him. A man who knows such glory, because of the support of his wife, will love and honor her more deeply than either of them could otherwise imagine.

I never want to ask my wife to be less than she is, for to do so would be to fault the way God has made her to provide the support I need. In the same regard, she should never deny or disregard the unique gifts God has given her to make me and our home more of what he intends. Love for our children and her spouse should keep her from the mere selfish exercise of her gifts. At the same time, however, this love should encourage her to find avenues for her talents and interests that enrich her life and, through her, enrich us all.

A friend recently sank into the classic male stereotype by refusing to ask directions after he had made a wrong turn to a vacation destination. His wife tried to help by grabbing a map from the glove compartment. She quickly spotted the road missed and began to give directions to get the family back on course—only to be interrupted by a teenage son in the backseat. "Hey, Mom, you can't tell Dad what to do," he said. "Remember what the Bible says: 'Wives are to suppress.'"

The mother quickly reminded her child that the Bible also says, "Children, honor your father *and* mother," and that the word his chauvinistic little mind was searching for was "submit." There was some humor in the situation, but also sadness. Already in this young man's thought, the biblical concept of submission had become synonymous with suppression. He had confused the exercise of a wife's abilities for the benefit of another with the repression of her knowledge despite the needs of another. Though these would seem to be concepts so opposed that they could scarcely be compared, such confusion regularly occurs in our culture, churches, and homes. Clarity comes when we consider the goodness God intends to promote through wives who meet their biblical responsibilities—and the dignity that is theirs as a result.

five

A Woman's Dignity
The Care of Another

thought that I had spoken so carefully. In the morning session of the conference I had spelled out not only the authority Scripture ascribes to husbands but also their duty to use that authority selflessly for the good of their wives and families. I reminded husbands that God's mandate to love their wives as Christ loved the church meant that they should never use their position for personal advantage, passivity, or bullying. Later in the day I spoke to wives about their need to submit, not as meek and mindless mice, but by making full use of their gifts for the support of the husbands God commits to their care. I meant to encourage and strengthen, but for at least one woman my words were deeply wounding.

She stood on the periphery of the crowd that came to ask questions after I had finished speaking. She waited more than half an hour until the rest of the crowd had dispersed. Then she stepped forward.

Professionally dressed and confident in bearing, she exuded business acumen and ability. When she spoke, she was articulate and she kept her voice level, but there was no mistaking her frustration. With her eyes fixed on mine, she said, "Why is it you cannot see that by telling wives they must submit their gifts to the support of their husbands, you make women second class? I don't care how nicely you state it and how kind you are trying to be. Once you make women subservient to men, you devalue us and perpetuate our oppression. Somebody must tell you that when you give these talks, you rob women of the dignity God gives them."

I respect her concern and know that she speaks for many other women. In an age of feminism, spousal abuse, two-income households, equal opportunity laws, and gender-neutral political agendas, it is hard to accept any words—even those of Scripture—that may appear to demean women. As a husband and father of daughters, I too find detestable any perspective that devalues the worth and significance of the women I love. My antipathy toward such ideas is not merely a result of family sentiment but a consequence of the biblical teaching that each person loved by God is infinitely precious to him. There is no difference in the value God places on individuals. He gave his Son to die on the cross to rescue each of us from an eternity without him.[1]

If God loves and values each person without variation, we may wonder how the Bible could teach that a wife should submit to her husband. The answer resides in these understandings: (1) the requirements of submission are not limited to one class of persons, and (2) the requirements of submission do not change the value of individuals even when their duties vary.

In heaven's accounting, persons are not valued according to the level of authority they possess but according to God's infinite, equal, and unconditional love. Our purposes vary but our value does not. For example, an elder with authority in a local church is not of more value or significance to God than the newest child member. Their duties vary, and God surely has different expectations for how they should express their differing gifts, but neither is of less significance. In fact the Bible says, "Those parts of the body [i.e., the church] that seem to be weaker are indispensable.

. . . God has combined the members of the body and has given greater honor to the parts that lacked it, so that there should be no division in the body, but that its parts should have equal concern for each other" (1 Cor. 12:22–25). Precisely because God has varied his design for the way individuals will carry out his purposes, each has special dignity. Eternal purposes, not earthly position, indicate why each person is of equal importance to God. God reveals these purposes to us so that we will share his perspective as we evaluate our own significance and as we deal with each other.

The Esteem of a Christian Wife

Because biblical submission requires the expression of one's gifts on behalf of another, dignity as well as duty resides in the expectations God has for wives. Initially this dignity results from understanding that the obligation to express gifts indicates that God has divine purpose for women in marriage. To see how biblical submission grants this dignity requires precise examination of the Bible's wording about a wife's duties compared to the obligations of others.

A Closer Look

A close look at the Bible's words about wifely submission may initially be shocking. In one key passage usually translated, "Wives, submit to your husbands" (Eph. 5:22), the word *submit* actually does not appear in the best early manuscripts of the Bible.[2] The very word we are so ready to debate is not even present in this verse. However, the absence of the word does not negate a wife's calling. With inspired genius the apostle's word choice not only underscores the necessity of a wife's biblical submission to her husband, it also confirms her dignity.

The word *submit* does appear in the verse preceding the directives for wives. Here the apostle concludes his general instruction on how to live a Spirit-filled life that honors God by saying that

Christians should, "Submit to one another out of reverence for Christ" (Eph. 5:21). Then these words follow: "Wives, to your husbands." There is no question that the apostle intends for wives to apply the submission instruction, just given, to their relationship with their husbands, even if the word *submit* does not appear in this verse. There is also no question, however, that wives are only the first group to whom the mandate of self-sacrifice or submission applies. Children and servants[3] are also reminded to submit to those in authority over them.

Accompanying these instructions to those who must submit to authority are commands for those in authority. In obedience to God, husbands must sacrifice their own interests to those under their care, as must parents and masters. To keep the lines of authority clear, neither apostle specifically tells husbands to submit to their wives.[4] However, using strong language and the Bible's most powerful analogy, the apostles consistently remind husbands that they must use their authority for the benefit of their wives in the way that Christ sacrificed his prerogatives for the good of his people (Eph. 5:25; 1 Peter 2:21–3:7).

A Common Denominator

Everyone must sacrifice for someone. Wives, children, and slaves must submit to husbands, parents, and masters. Husbands, parents, and masters must serve the needs of those for whom they are responsible in accord with Christ's example of sacrifice for those under his care. The flow of the passage, thus, unfolds by addressing people as follows:

Submit to one another . . .

- Wives, to your husbands as to the Lord (Eph. 5:22–24, 33)
- Husbands, love your wives, as the Lord gave himself for the church (5:25–33)
- Children, obey your parents (6:1–3)
- Fathers, do not exasperate your children (6:4)
- Servants, obey masters properly from your heart (6:5–8)

- Masters, treat servants with respect and fairness since you are slaves of Christ (6:9)

Each person must offer whatever gifts, rights, or authority he (or she) has in service to the good of another for the building up of Christ's kingdom.

The reason this structure confirms the dignity of a Christian wife is that it proves that her submission does not automatically lessen her value or diminish her status in the kingdom. *All* Christians are to submit themselves to the good of others God has placed in their lives. Although the apostle clearly assigns differing purposes to husbands and wives, he just as clearly exempts no one from the Christ-like attitudes and actions required of everyone:

> Do nothing out of selfish ambition or vain conceit, but in humility consider others better than yourselves. Each of you should look not only to your own interests, but also to the interests of others.
>
> Your attitude should be the same as that of Christ Jesus: Who, being in very nature God, did not consider equality with God something to be grasped, but made himself nothing, taking the very nature of a servant, being made in human likeness. And being found in appearance as a man, he humbled himself and became obedient to death—even death on a cross!
>
> Philippians 2:3–8

God's call for selfless sacrifice to all who honor him makes willing submission to others' best interests the common denominator of Christian experience, not the reducer of personal worth. Identifying this common denominator provides the initial means we have to answer from Scripture those who question the concept of submission, such as the professional businesswoman mentioned at the outset of this chapter. Her concern that the Bible sets up the oppression of women is not foolish, given the way our world tends to equate authority with value and importance. These concerns must be addressed with Scripture's full picture and the reminder that the world's values are not heaven's.

We must acknowledge that the Bible does tell wives to submit to their husbands, but this is in a context where husbands are also required to honor God's standards for the exercise of their authority, using it for the good of their wives. Further, we must affirm that the Bible requires wives to obey whatever their husbands may require that is not contrary to God's Word, but this is in the context of the requirement that husbands sacrifice their interests for the good of their wives.

There are levels of authority in the family, but because all persons subject themselves to some higher authority and to another's good, the submission required of wives gives them obligations as significant as those of any other person. This mutual significance levels rather than stratifies worth. Further, since each person must live for the other, each affirms the greater worth of the other in terms of the priorities of life.

Because each person has a heavenly mandate, all are part of a divine purpose. Each bears the image of God (Gen. 1:27). Each was deemed precious enough by God to be purchased from sin's condemnation by the Son's blood (Col. 1:20–22). Each of us has equal spiritual status now that we are clothed in Christ's righteousness (Gal. 3:26–28). Each will receive a heavenly inheritance (1 Peter 3:7). Thus, though God does not assign men and women identical responsibilities in marriage, Scripture allows neither to be treated disrespectfully (see Eph. 5:33 and 1 Peter 3:7).[5]

The Bible frees both men and women from the human grids that use power and accomplishment to determine worth. God removes the price tags, based on personal comparisons and performance, we put on ourselves and replaces them with the knowledge of our infinite value because we are faithful to God's designs that accomplish his eternal purposes.

Janette Alexander, wife of the great nineteenth-century theologian Archibald Alexander, was renowned within her own family for her sensitive interpretations of Scripture. Although she lacked the technical training her husband possessed, her walk with God nevertheless gave her special understanding of the Spirit's intentions in his Word. When Janette Alexander's son had also become a scholar of note who devoted himself to writing commentaries on the books of the Bible, he often sought his mother's insights. He said, "Her common sense, in certain matters of this kind, was worth more than all the commentaries in the world."[6]

The son's comment was a wonderful compliment to his mother but it also allows us to see from God's perspective his purposes that determine value. Janette Alexander was not the founding professor of a seminary as was her husband. She did not have the technical training her husband provided numerous students, including their son. She never had the worldwide reputation for theological insight her husband achieved. Yet she gave her husband buoyant support and their children godly care. She is credited with helping her husband acquire the plainness of speech, joy, and compassion that made students so respect him as a teacher. And when her son produced commentaries used by hundreds of preachers to prepare sermons for countless thousands of people, he sought the wisdom of her heart.

Should we try to determine who did the greater work—Archibald Alexander or Janette Alexander—the arguments would be endless. They should be. Seen from heaven's perspective both persons in this marriage fulfilled a special purpose that had innumerable eternal consequences the human mind cannot begin to conceive nor account. To try to place relative value on their respective accomplishments would defy our mental capabilities and deny the unique and necessary contribution of each to heaven's purposes. Husband and wife submitted to the good of the other and to the design of God, which he rewarded by granting them great usefulness in his eternal scheme.

We could multiply the examples many times to illustrate that the varying designs God has for our lives have nothing to do with the value he places on us. For instance, consider which of these persons are more important: Billy Graham or the mother who raised him, the president of a seminary or the elderly woman who prays for him, the choir that sings or the organist that accompanies, the husband who leads or the wife who supports him. The way our lives and efforts are interwoven should teach us that the one who submits to another to enable the work of God to progress is as important as the one who does other aspects of the work.

When Ann Judson accompanied her husband, Adoniram, to India, she could not have predicted the importance of her role in reaching millions with the message of Jesus—nor could she have anticipated the degree of submission such usefulness would require. When tensions arose between the governments of England and India, Western missionaries were imprisoned as foreign enemies.

Adoniram was thrown with other prisoners in a cell so small that some had to stand while others took their turn sleeping. They were deprived of sanitation and water, and under the oppressive heat, the stench became sickening. Even these conditions were not cruel enough for the captors who inflicted further punishment by hanging prisoners, including Adoniram, from their thumbs until the heat and pain broke many of the will to live.

Adoniram survived on words from his wife, Ann. Descending into the squalor of the prison, and enduring the jeers of the guards, she visited her husband when others' fears made them abandon their spouses. On her visits she ladled courage to her husband with eyes that poured love through the prison bars and she refreshed his soul with her words. "Do not give up, Adoniram," Ann said. "God will give us the victory." When hope died in others, those oft-repeated words kept the missionary alive.

Then the visits stopped. For days and then months Ann failed to appear. Whereas anticipation of her visits once kept him alive, now concern for her condition drove Adoniram to make it through each day. When changes in the government led eventually to his release, he began a desperate search for his wife.

Adoniram soon learned that the deprivations of being considered a foreign enemy had taken their toll on his wife as well. Ann was dying. As he approached the tent she had been assigned in her illness, Adoniram came on a child so filthy and poorly clothed that he did not at first recognize her as his own daughter. Inside the tent the conditions were no better. Her body shrunken by disease and malnutrition, Ann lay without movement on tattered blankets. The illness had taken her hair and warped her features so that she was barely recognizable, except for the eyes that still poured out love and the words of support that were uttered for the last time. "Do not give up, Adoniram," she said. "God will give us the victory."

Adoniram Judson took his dying wife's words of encouragement as a charge from God. The millions who have since learned of Jesus as a result of his ministry are the spiritual children of Ann

Judson. As she lived and died supporting her husband, Ann's own life and ennobling love fulfilled a divine purpose of eternal value.

In Christ's kingdom submission does not lessen the standing of believers, it confirms their significance. Submission will not call every person to a mission field, but it gives every life a mission. Through the sacrifice of personal interests, we fulfill God's purposes for our (and others') lives and thus confirm our vital role in God's eternal plan. Christians' responsibilities vary in fulfilling this plan, but their value does not. As Paul says elsewhere, "The eye cannot say to the hand, 'I don't need you!'" (1 Cor. 12:21). A wife who supports her husband through a crisis at work or teaches her children to honor his authority or yields to his decision during a family impasse concedes no inferior status. Instead, she affirms God's call on her life and rightly presumes that her role is as vital for the results God intends as that of the husband she aids.

Being equal in worth does not require our being the same in function. To conclude otherwise would ultimately require us to reason that Christ became an inferior in the Godhead when he submitted himself to the Father, or that the Spirit deserves less glory because he carries out the desires of the Son. Such reasoning is, of course, heretical. The persons of the Trinity are equally divine despite their distinctly different functions and purposes.[7] By his Trinitarian nature our God has made it abundantly clear that equal value does not require identical roles.[8]

The Glory of a Christian Wife

The dignity of a Christian wife shows not only in the sacrificial calling that she shares with all God's people but also in the glory of the purpose God grants her. To understand the dignity of this purpose, it may be helpful to compare it to the goals for women our society sometimes advocates. In contrast to the biblical perspective that a woman fulfills heavenly purposes in honoring God's marriage design (even when those purposes may not be immediately evident), some modern perspectives shackle women to standards of income, title, and accomplishment as measurements of worth. The sadness of this perspective is that it teaches women that if they have not sufficiently risen in corporate stature or professional recognition, then their lives are worth less than the lives of those who have achieved more. Worth becomes directly tied to a row of figures in a bank book or a line of ink in a year-end report.

While the Bible offers no support for denying women equal opportunity in the workplace,[9] God clearly wants women (and men) to gauge their significance by matters of greater consequence than material possessions or passing praise (Matt. 16:26; 1 Tim. 6:17–19). When estimations of personal worth get linked to personal success or superior position, then one's dignity exists simply in comparison to the position of others. Because there are no guarantees in life, linking our significance to the material possessions and personal achievements we have, or hope to have, is dangerous at best. Still, the ultimate reason God cautions against tying our importance to our comparative affluence or position relates to factors much more certain than economic or relational setbacks.

A subtle, yet spiritually debilitating, change occurs in a woman when her dignity is measured by wealth, number of children, size of house, personal accomplishments, or a husband's prestige. Such measures turn a woman's attention from God's purposes to herself. The shift of focus deprives women of true dignity.

The indignity of this self-focus recently became apparent in an unlikely source. An avant-garde woman's magazine reviewed the current crop of books written for modern women. The reviewer first noted that early feminist books had been about how women could achieve access to power and money. But in assessing the current books, she concluded:

> Feminism is no longer a battle for equal opportunity in a male-dominated society, but a kind of 12-step recovery program for wounded women. . . . "There is an endless appetite for self-help books. . . ." They do not offer women still struggling in an unfair world any clarion call to arms. Instead they urge women to redefine their inner lives.[10]

This review was written by an advocate of modern feminism. How sad (and revealing) that, at least in this reviewer's estimation, a cause that began with such altruistic rhetoric and pleas for justice, equality, and dignity now is but another journey into me-ism.[11] Whether feminist efforts return to seeking justice for women or stay focused on inner healing cannot be predicted. What is plain even to those in the women's movement is the indignity of a cause focused on pouring one's life and demands into the vain, cloying pursuit of "what's-in-it-for-me."

Whether it is a man or woman, no one is so detestable as an individual who is driven by selfishness, and nothing is so ennobling as a life given in service and sacrifice for others. We sense these truths in the comic book life of a Donald Trump, who gains power and wealth at the expense of our respect, and we see the opposite in the life of a Mother Teresa, who received the honor of the world and its rulers though she had nothing. The relative glory even our society assigns these individuals enables us to gauge the dignity God grants to the wife who submits herself to the good of her husband and family. The Bible says that they will rise up and call her blessed (Prov. 31:28). Her dignity is assured in the health, beauty, and blessing of the ones to whom she gives herself. Her glory resides in her unwillingness to be driven by any priorities other than God's. Heaven is reflected in her focus on others.

The Church's Affirmation

Affirmation of the value and glory of a wife who lives for another should be one of the great ministries of the church. Sadly we seem to have trouble offering this kind of ministry. Some branches of the church seem so caught up in fighting for women's rights that they sound little different from the secular voices that make self-fulfillment life's highest aim. As a result, biblical marriage and family priorities get lost in a shuffle for power and position that seems to have little to do with the selfless life Christ urged. Other branches of the church are so threatened by the various women's movements that their chief response to women seems to be to keep them "in their place." As a consequence, churches can become much more facile at attacking capable women than at affirming them and seeking to discern how their gifts may be biblically employed for Christ's purposes.

Because we have trouble remembering that submission is an arranging of one's gifts under the purposes of God and is a disposition to yield to authority rather than a universal code of behaviors, we create tensions that needlessly deny women the opportunities to serve God that he desires. We damage our own wives and daughters as a result. My wife says to me, "Bryan, it doesn't matter what I do, there are people in our church who will accuse me of not fulfilling my proper role. If I devote myself entirely to family care, some women in the church will say that I have abandoned my potential in the workplace and am contributing to the subjugation of my own daughters. If I work outside the home— even part-time—others will accuse me of forsaking Scripture and giving in to cultural pressures. For women in the church today, all choices are attackable."

In the face of such conflict and confusion, the church must speak clearly of the nobility of a life lived for the good of another. Jesus said anyone who follows him must "deny himself" (Matt. 16:24; Mark 8:34; Luke 9:23). More than a call to an occasional act of charity, this is a charge to put God's priorities above our own on a daily basis. We are to live according to God's design with the faith that there is nothing more valuable or important that we can do. This means my own calling is to assure my wife that there is nothing more precious to me, and nothing more valuable to our family, than her submission to her biblical responsibilities in our home.

The Husband's Affirmation

A Christian woman said to me recently, "I understand why so many women struggle with what the Bible says about submission but I have never struggled with submitting to my husband because he lets me know how much he respects me." That husband's life is what Scripture requires men to live.

The apostle Peter says, "Husbands . . . be considerate as you live with your wives and treat them with respect . . ." (1 Peter 3:7).

These words require that I let my wife know how much I respect the way she has submitted herself to the good of our family, even when the choices have been difficult. I need to remember that it caused no little consternation for her college instructors when she did not pursue a promising concert career that would have intruded on our church ministry. I should relish the creative ways that she has used her musical gifts to bring glory to God and good to our family throughout our married lives. When my early jobs brought meager financial support to our family, she taught music lessons for extra income. For many years she has led children and adult choirs, often without pay, to share with our children and our church her love of music that glorifies God. She has performed countless solos, hymn accompaniments, Christmas programs, and Easter cantatas for the pure joy of sharing her music with others. She has even let me croak Broadway tunes with her at our home piano. All this she has done while raising four children to love the Lord—the greatest instruments of her praise.

Depending on the ages of our children, our financial needs, and the demands of my job, Kathy has varied the allocation of her time and energies to occupations outside our home. Yet she has never wavered in submitting her own interests to the needs of those God has entrusted to her care. In a confusing age others may question her choices, but I respect them—and her. I pray that she will never doubt the glorious regard that I have for her because heaven itself honors her support of her husband and home.

Heaven's Honor

The Puritan preacher John Angell James sought to summarize the glory of a wife who lives according to God's priorities in these words:

> Man is neither safe in himself, nor profitable to others, when he lives dissociated from that benign influence which is to be found in woman's presence and character. . . . But it is not woman . . . separated from those divine teachings which make all hearts wise, that can lay claim to the exercise of such influence. But when she

adds to the traits of sympathy, forbearance, and warm affection, which characterize her, the strength and wisdom of a well-cultivated intellect, and the still higher attributes of religious faith and holy love, it is not easy to limit the good she may do in all situations, and in all periods of life.[12]

Historically when Scripture has been rightly interpreted and the church has been rightly motivated, women have been granted honor. Present-day Christians must take care that cultural forces do not press us away from this biblical perspective. Even in churches where we claim to hold dear the Scriptures that speak of the preciousness of women in God's family economy, women consistently report that they are the object of the jests, jibes, and insensitivity of men. We may understand (but cannot accept) the explanation that biblically conservative churches are under siege from the feminist forces of our society. If we really think, however, that we will uphold biblical priorities by embarrassing, intimidating, and demoralizing those God places among us, then we reveal our insecurity more than we promote orthodoxy. We cannot expect Christian wives to treasure the duties God has designed for them if the church does not vigorously defend the dignity of women's responsibilities and give honor to those who assume them.

In the summer of 1996 Joan Hollinshead took her husband, Tom, for a walk in a nearby park. Seriously disabled by a stroke at an age that was decades before such catastrophes usually strike, Tom was grateful for the outing after months of rehabilitation. To add to their fun, Joan also took along the dog that delighted Tom. The three slowly ambled down the mile-long walking path circling the park, but the challenge was still greater than they anticipated.

Halfway around the park Tom's legs began to tremble. His strength evaporated and he could go no farther. Joan knew Tom needed medical attention quickly but she had no way to get him back to their car. Supporting him even a short distance to a place where he could sit had proved awkward with the now anxious dog dancing around their feet. Not having alternatives, Joan prepared to leave Tom to go get help. In the desperation of the moment she fought her fears with a quickly voiced prayer. "Dear Lord," she said, "I don't know what to do. Please send your angels to help us."

When she lifted her head from prayer, a policeman on a motorcycle was coming down the path. The officer quickly summoned help and the emergency passed.

Then Joan asked the policeman, "What made you come down this walking path on your motorcycle? I have never seen a policeman in this part of the park."

The officer replied, "We have wanted a greater police presence in the park, so the city council just authorized us to patrol these paths. My ride tonight was our very first patrol."

Joan thought, *Mr. Policeman, you may have thought the authorization came from the city council, but I think it came from a higher authority.*

That day in a special way heaven honored the support a Christian wife gave her husband. What I wish for her and for every wife who gives herself every day for the good of her spouse—in a thousand less dramatic ways—is the knowledge that heaven honors each gift. God's own glory is reflected in the wife who lives for another.

six

A Woman's Desire

The Honor of Another

An old commercial for car wax depicts a young woman preparing to sell her car. Aged and dull, the vehicle that she has used for years holds no more allure for her. Yet when she uses the "miracle" wax to put shine back on the vehicle's finish, the new glow revives the woman's old affection for her car. She throws away the "For Sale" sign, and drives away, happy again in a car she treasures anew.

Though silly, the commercial speaks truly of the way our hearts function. What we make precious to ourselves, we love. When we invest ourselves in the satisfaction, security, and development of other persons, we do more than build their self-esteem. We add to our esteem of them. By contributing to another's sense of worth, we also delight in that person more. Applied to marriage, these truths become the threads that knit and repair relationships between husbands and wives.

When a woman nourishes, nurtures, and affirms her spouse, her love for him deepens. The regard she gives her husband not only expresses her love but builds it. When such regard diminishes, love itself fails. For this reason, the Bible instructs that a wife search for the affection that deepens biblical love, not in the attributes of her husband but in the desires of her heart (1 Peter 3:1–6). This instruction resonates with the deeper truth that because we most deeply love what we regard most highly, a wife longs to think highly of her husband because intuitively she knows her capacity to love resides in that regard. What the Bible commands only harmonizes with what an unselfish and unwounded heart affirms.

To Respect Her Husband

As the apostle Paul concludes comments on marriage in the Book of Ephesians, he reminds men to "love" their wives, but he tells women to "respect" their husbands (6:33). Here the apostle seems to be dealing with each gender at the weak points of our relational tendencies. Often a man's great temptation is to use the power of his position and physique to enforce dictatorial rule or to indulge passive self-absorption. A woman's parallel temptation is often to use the power of words and emotions to diminish a husband so that she has control. Paul allows neither "power play" by commanding men to love and women to respect their spouses.

The power of the forces the apostle seeks to curb were dramatically evident to Kathy and me early in our marriage. Our meager income required us to live in a cheap apartment in a poor part of town. There the paper-thin walls and floors of the housing complex gave us an ear-opening perspective on the way some people live. Given our sheltered suburban backgrounds, the vileness and violence so many of the families around us considered normal were shocking to us.

Most disconcerting for us were the habits of the minister's family that lived below us. Most of the fights between that husband and wife were about who was the better witness. We usually tried to ignore the shouts and slaps until he would choke her so that she could not respond. Then we would try to find some way to intervene. We dropped books on the floor to remind the couple we were present. We called on the phone and borrowed cups of sugar at very odd times just to distract them from each other. Occasionally we called the police.

The experience sickened us but it also matured us. As we listened to the husband and wife shout their way to the brutal climax of what became almost nightly conflicts, we began to recognize a pattern. The husband would get irritated with something his wife or children had said or done. He would shout his disapproval. The wife in turn would begin to criticize him with equal volume and at greater length for some shortcoming or failure. Her readiness to return the verbal assault surprised Kathy and me. We would sometimes turn to one another and say, "Why does she taunt him so? She knows he is going to hit her."

We did not know then what we have since learned about abusive homes: that as often as a man will try to dominate a woman with his strength, a woman will try to control a man with shame. The verbal criticism our downstairs neighbor directed at her husband was her tool to make her husband back down. Sometimes it worked—sometimes it did not.

Even if violence is not present (though too often it is), the various ways these spouses tried to control each other are the practices found in many marriages. Men often exert their control with intimidation or intransigence that are both expressions of power. Women may use a demeaning look, a cutting remark, an accusation, or some embarrassing reminder to diminish a man so he becomes less sure of himself and thus more controllable.

Sadly these factors often become cyclical. Insecure men react to their sense of being diminished by becoming more dominating. This in turn gives a wife more opportunity to needle and shame, which subsequently triggers more abuse. When this cycle is in effect to any degree, the marriage becomes a daily tug-of-war for power. Power may be expressed through intimidation or manipulation. Control measures may take the form of screaming or scheming, silence or secrecy, whining or withdrawal, violence or victimization. Whether the means are active or passive, the goal of each of these behaviors remains the same—keeping the other person under control.

115

For His Sake

Against all of these control mechanisms, the Bible crusades for a different ruling force: love (Eph. 5:1–2). Scripture does not allow a Christian husband the privilege to intimidate or ignore his wife to serve his own interests. The Bible does not give a Christian wife the right to diminish or shame her husband to get her way. God commands selfless care that excludes any striving for spousal control.

Early in our marriage my wife and I agreed not to belittle one another in public even in jest. Our agreement came after noticing how many of our friends used ridicule (often disguised in teasing) to get an edge over each other. Remarks about someone's appearance, reminders of a past embarrassment, or drawing attention to a dumb comment are standard ways that couples use polite conversation to corral each other's actions and attitudes. My wife and I actually enjoy teasing one another but we do not kid in a way that is demeaning for the sake of a laugh from others. I have to be honest with my wife and say simply that I need her respect.

Women may not recognize how much husbands are affected by their wives' respect—or lack of it. There have been moments in my life when I felt the only significant things I could claim as my own were the respect and love of my wife. When a church's leadership was convinced I was wrong, when I felt I had sacrificed my career for a cause everyone about me seemed to think was foolish, when others have made me doubt my own competence, when I have delivered an awful sermon, when I have been guilty of sin that I knew exposed the weakness of my faith—in each of those moments the respect of my wife has meant everything. She has loved me enough to look past my weaknesses, stupidities, and failures and see traits in me that she could still respect. Not only has her consistent respect secured our love; it has also given me confidence, strength, and courage. I could neither do nor be what I believe God requires were it not for my wife's consistent and faithful regard for me.

All husbands are strengthened by the respect of their wives. God has made men this way or he would not have commanded wives to be so careful to give their husbands this consideration. Men were made in need of a helper (Gen. 2:18). A wife who understands that God designed her husband with this need can rejoice that she is part of God's plan to bring support and wholeness to the man she loves. A wife who does not understand that God designed husbands to thrive through their wives' respect too often discovers that her husband finds other sources of the respect he requires.

Hollywood stereotypes to the contrary, my counseling experience indicates married men do not typically get involved in extramarital relationships with women more beautiful and sophisticated than their wives. Men have affairs with women who make them feel important, cherished, competent—in a word, respected. Often men in such affairs will acknowledge that they are involved with someone who does not "measure up" to their wives in beauty, intelligence, or social standing. Still, the man's need to be highly regarded by a woman drives him to one who knows him less well but treats him more highly than his wife.

A man's need never excuses his betrayal, nor does his guilt necessarily imply his wife's neglect. But the woman who loves her spouse and wants to help guard him from sin strives to make her regard for her husband his lifeline to self-respect. Staying interested in a husband's career, rejoicing in his successes, cheerleading his ambitions, listening to his dreams, honoring his decisions, admiring his physical appearance, and making it a joyous offering of love to overlook flaws in each of these areas, are powerful seductions available to every wife.

For Her Sake

I do not want to give the impression, however, that a wife should give her husband respect merely to serve his ego. As much as I appreciate her care, I love my wife too much to want her regard if giving it would damage her. Of greater consideration to me, and to Scripture, is the effect giving respect has on one's own heart. Susan Hunt offers this poignant account by an unnamed writer:

Before marriage I was attracted to my husband's strong personality. After marriage this same personality overwhelmed me. I began

117

believing the lie that Eve believed in the Garden—I could not be fulfilled doing it God's way. I believed the lies that I would have to fight for my rights and that it was my responsibility to destroy my husband's ego, so I did everything I could to belittle him. I corrected him in public. I rarely expressed admiration or appreciation. In trying to destroy his pride, I was destroying his manhood and elevating my own pride. I convinced myself that when he changed, I would be a great wife. I was less and less interested in him. There were no feelings of affection or love. I would rather have gone to an execution than to bed with my husband. I turned off all the music and wore flannel nightgowns. I resented the fact that my husband was so needy, ignoring the truth that perfect Adam also had needs.[1]

The husband is not the only one who benefits from the respect a godly wife offers; she benefits too. The respect a wife offers her husband is a key to the deeper levels of marital bliss for which her own heart yearns. The more she treasures her husband, the more precious a woman will find their union and the more rewarding their relationship will become to her. The woman who longs for the bonds of love finds her deepest satisfaction is providing the support that secures the relationship for which she longs. Conversely the woman who does not offer her husband respect denies herself the potential for intimacy.

In some measure these principles apply to men as well as women. A man who does not consider his wife worthy of his honor will also lose his desire for true intimacy with her. God requires each marriage partner to respect the other. The apostle Peter writes, "Husbands, in the same way be considerate as you live with your wives, and treat them with respect as the weaker partner and as heirs with you of the gracious gift of life, so that nothing will hinder your prayers" (1 Peter 3:7).

The obligations of mutual regard are not less for either spouse, but these obligations do vary. Peter's words remind us that each husband should respect his wife for the tenderness and sensitivity she brings to their home, for the support she offers that gives her a right to inherit the same spiritual blessings as he, and for the opportunity his care of her provides for him to cultivate his own spiritual relationship with the Lord. The Bible requires men to discern reasons to respect their wives because love and honor are inextricably linked. The women the Bible presents as most desirable are those most highly honored by their husbands (cf. Song of Sol. 7:1–9; Prov. 31:10–31). Men are attracted to those they honor and are repulsed by those they disrespect. Physical attraction, though powerful, will not maintain a relationship in which mutual respect has died. The women whom the Bible most highly honors for the love they have for their husbands are also those who respect their spouses (1 Peter 3:5–6).

As I write these words, the marriages of some of my friends are coming unglued. At almost any time in my adult life, I could say this. The causes are too numerous to count, but consistent in almost all of these sad scenarios are years of battle for control of the home. The couples presently struggling are successful and blessed with beautiful children. All the spouses consider themselves committed Christians. Yet, despite these wonderful gifts, these couples' homes have become battlegrounds for power, with each personal gift and talent a weapon in the war. Financial success and credit accounts allow each spouse to be independent and self-indulgent. Children's activities become excuses for one parent to ignore the other, or children's antics become reasons to blame each other. Because they are intelligent and articulate, the couples are able to use arguments, excuses, and jests that back a spouse into a corner. Each spouse uses the faith commitment of the other like a flashlight to expose inconsistencies or to reveal guilt that will cause concession in an argument.

These people will all stand before the Lord one day to give an account of their role in these domestic battles for control. Husbands will need to explain why their leadership turned self-serving or severe. Wives must answer whether they honored their husband as the Bible requires.

All Christian women must remember that the corrupted values of our world tempt each heart to desire control. After Adam and Eve sinned, God said that from then on women would desire their husbands' position and dominance.[2] God's redeeming influence in the heart of a woman does not make her want equal or greater dominance with a man, but restores in her an appreciation for the headship God designed for her husband. This means real peace cannot come to the domestic battleground of any marriage until each partner seeks to serve rather than to sway the other. The service that brings a wife fulfillment begins with recognition that the love for which her heart longs cannot flourish without the respect for her husband that God requires.

Every day I try to tell my wife that I love her. I know that she delights to hear it, though, candidly, I do not have the same depth of appreciation for these words that she does. My expression of love for her touches something deep in her heart that I (as a sometimes less-than-sensitive man) do not fully comprehend. I say the words because I love bringing her joy, not because I entirely understand how or why they transmit that joy.

I wish that women understood that a man's awareness of his wife's respect is the firm ground on which he plants his feet to meet life's challenges. This meets an important need of a man in the same way that a husband's assurances of his love provide a wife security, renewal, and comfort for the trials of life. The firmer the ground of his wife's respect, the more able the husband is to react with proper strength or tenderness to the challenges at hand. When he is less sure of his wife's regard, he is more likely to seek security in other things or persons. The respect a wife shows her husband secures her marriage in ways more powerful than most women (or men) fully comprehend.

The apostle Paul spoke with great understanding of men and women when he concluded, "Each [man] must love his wife as he loves himself, and the wife must respect her husband" (Eph. 5:33). The words remind husbands and wives to express care for one another in the ways that touch each other's heart most deeply. When a woman senses that her marriage has yet to know its full riches or when her relationship with her husband has grown cold, God offers this powerful tool of help and healing: Wives, respect your husbands.

To Reverence Her Husband

God reveals the importance of a woman's attitude toward her husband in the word he uses to tell us how she should express her regard. Some versions of the Bible seem almost to try to tiptoe past our modern sensibilities, saying, ". . . the wife must *respect* her husband" (Eph. 5:33). The word translated "respect" actually comes from the same term the apostle Paul used a few sentences earlier to say we must "reverence" Christ (Eph. 5:21). The apostle uses this word to communicate godly fear or holy awe.

The apostle's language causes me to remember a woman in our church who was seeking to divorce her husband without biblical cause. When church leaders urged her to find new cause to love her husband, she replied, "Love him?! I can't even stomach him. Just the thought of him makes me ill." I can only imagine how much stronger her reaction would have been if we had urged her to reverence him!

We can easily make sense of the word *reverence* when it refers to Christ. We understand how and why we are to honor our Savior. But why would Paul say a wife should *reverence* her husband?

The Reasons for Reverence

We cannot say with certainty why Paul uses the term *reverence.* Surely one reason is that he wants to emphasize the regard due biblical headship. None should slight what the Bible says we should revere. Both the head of the home and the one married to him should recognize that by using *reverence* to describe how a wife should regard her husband, the Bible identifies headship as a holy office in the home. The husband assumes serious responsibilities in light of the holy obligations of such an office, as does the wife in terms of both her attitudes and her actions toward him.

Another possible reason the apostle uses the word is to underscore that the husband, as the spiritual head of the home, is the one who must give account to God for the spiritual nurture of his family. The wife who has the vision to perceive what a husband's position requires will understand why such responsibility inspires reverence. We might compare her response to that of a young Olympian's parents who are nearly awestruck by the amazing achievements of their own child who performs before millions under the scrutiny of human judges. So a wife, who sees with spiritual eyes, perceives the breathtaking glory of her husband's performance of his spiritual duties before both the hosts of heaven and the Judge of the universe. Every husband is accountable to God for the spiritual guidance he gives his family. The holiness and gravity of a husband's obligations are so awesome that they require honor, even though he carries them out imperfectly.

The Resources for Reverence

The husband's certain imperfections provide an even more probable reason for the Bible's use of *reverence* to describe how a wife should relate to her husband. The term points a wife back to the source of her esteem for her husband—and reminds her the source is *not* in him.

The word *reverence* at the conclusion of the apostle's discussion of marriage echoes his introduction. There Paul encourages us to order our relationships out of reverence for Christ (Eph. 5:21). By repeating this theme in the final instruction to wives, the apostle says in effect, The reverence you have for your husband should find its source not in who he is, nor in what he does, nor in how deserving he is. The attitude to which God calls you is rooted in your relationship with the Savior. Thus the honor you show your husband should come from the desire you have to please God.

Rooting a wife's regard for her husband in her relationship with the Savior answers a question I recognize some readers have had since the opening of this chapter: What should I do if my husband is undeserving of my respect, much less my reverence? For many the question will come out of deep pain. For others the question is an honest evaluation of a husband's condition. For still others the question stems from an unwillingness to be bound by God's Word. Whether the reason for asking comes from good motives or ill, the answer remains the same. God requires a wife to honor her husband, not because of the goodness he possesses but because of the grace he needs.

Though some men may be worthy of their wives' respect, none are worthy of their wives' reverence. God's command that a wife give such undeserved regard requires us to consider the honor as an unmerited gift rather than an earned deference.

Just as a husband's qualities do not ultimately kindle his wife's respect or reverence, neither should his faults quench them. This does not mean that a wife should approve of her husband's errors or participate in his ungodliness. She should, however, recognize that in service to her Savior, she is a conduit of grace to her spouse as long as God binds her to him. A husband experiences God's unmerited favor through the undeserved honor a wife gives him personally, regardless of his frailties and failures. Respecting the characteristics of a spouse that can be honored, forgiving the flaws that cannot be honored, and caring for the man regardless of his dishonor—all these attitudes in some measure bless the man, but in greater measure they reverence God (see 1 Peter 3:9).

The most quoted line from the classic movie *Chariots of Fire* was Eric Liddell's explanation of why he ran. "Because when I run," he said, "I feel God's pleasure." Those words echoed in my mind when a distraught husband sought release from his wife's love. He had lost his job, spent his last dollar on diversions to make him forget, and had returned home expecting his wife to add her scorn to the weight of his self-defeat. Instead, she told him that she loved him. He collapsed sobbing into a chair in the living room, and as I looked on, she placed a hand on his shoulder and for the next half hour reminded him of the good she loved in him.

The words the wife spoke did as much to fill her heart with care as they did to rebuild the young man's self-respect. She told him how she admired his sensitivity and care for their children. She reminded him of the ways he made her laugh and of moments their family treasured. She listed the people who believed in him. Simply by recounting what she did respect in this terribly flawed man, the wife's eyes glistened with renewed love. He knew that he was undeserving of this kind of love. At one point he objected to her words, "I don't want you to love me so much." She responded simply, "God does." She gave her husband respect not only because he needed it, but because she knew God delighted in it.

This divine-source motivation permeates all of the apostle Paul's thought about marriage and takes priority over all other reasons that he says we should honor one another. His startling command for wives to hold their husbands in "holy awe" at the end of this discussion is actually the bloom of thoughts planted at its beginning: "Be imitators of God, therefore, as dearly loved children and live a life of love, just as Christ loved us and gave himself up for us as a fragrant offering and sacrifice to God" (Eph. 5:1–2). The confidence and joy we take from the Lord's love is the strength and motive for our own. Wives are to reverence their husbands (and husbands are to give themselves for their wives) out of reverence for what Christ has done for us. Ultimately all of us are to be continuing Christ's sacrificial work in each other out of love for him. Just as Jesus' sacrifice was a fragrance that pleased God, so our ultimate desire to fulfill our marital responsibility lies in the knowledge that it too brings pleasure to the God of grace.

I sensed some of this divine pleasure at a Valentine social my wife and I recently attended. Those present at the banquet took much delight in listening to an older couple sing their own version of "Do You Love Me" from the musical *Fiddler on the Roof.* At the point of the song where the stage characters are supposed to sing, "After twenty-five years it's nice to know [that you love me]," this couple substituted their own marriage's stats and sang, "After forty-eight years it's nice to know." In a church dominated by young marriages that have not yet stood the test of years, the enduring love of this couple was more than endearing. It was inspiring. When they hit the last notes of the song, the room exploded in a standing ovation as we cheered for a love that had so powerfully encouraged us and had so radiantly persevered in them.

We were about to discover there was more for them to endure. Just a few minutes later their forty-one-year-old son also went on the stage to tell us about his current battle with cancer and the hope that he still claims as a result of his parents' life of faith. After the social, I spoke to the parents privately in a remote hallway of the church where we were gathering our coats. I told the couple that I had been surprised by their son's cancer report. They said that the news was only days old to them as well. There had been no history or warning signs to prepare them—just an out-of-the-blue telephone call: "Mom and Dad, I have cancer."

As they told me this account of their beloved son, the recentness of the news with its shock, grief, and fear welled in the couple. The man, usually so stoic, never showing weakness, could not keep tears from his eyes. When his wife saw his pain and the embarrassment of his tears, she touched his arm. It was such a small and subtle gesture, and yet I could almost see the strength flow from her as the man then collected himself and spoke again of their faith in God's care.

The wife, I am sure, wanted to cry as much as (if not more than) her husband. The tears would have been far more typical of her, and she had no less need to be comforted by him. Yet in that moment he needed her strength and in that reassuring touch she sacrificed the expression of her own grief to minister to his pain. In their oneness she knew just how to help him and how to preserve his respect in the midst of her own hurting. The simple gesture represented a duty of deep love, a dignifying of him that dignified her, and a desire to serve her husband that had been nurtured through a lifetime of serving God.

Who witnessed this wife's giving of herself in that caring touch in the hall? I did, and maybe one or two others, but for her I again heard applause—another standing ovation. This applause known only to the heart was exploding from the portals of heaven as its hosts rejoiced for a wife who in those moments submitted her right to grieve to her husband's need for support. I hope with her spiritual ears she heard it too. On that day I pray that she sensed heaven's regard for the beauty of her service. On this day may you who read these words also know and claim the eternal value, scriptural glory, and personal delight of every wife who submits to her husband out of reverence for the Lord.

Part 3

Sacrificial Partners
Shared Love

Submit to one another out of reverence for Christ.

Ephesians 5:21

In her book *The True Woman,* Susan Hunt tells of a mutual friend of ours named Rosalie Cassels.[1] Rosalie has been a member of the Rosehill Presbyterian Church in Columbia, South Carolina, since her father began the church as a Sunday school class for poor children more than eighty years ago.

In her early adult years, Rosalie devoted herself to training women to serve the Lord. She became a leader in the organization of women's efforts and many other concerns of her denomination. Because of her husband's success in business, she was also able to afford repeated travels to the mission field to support missionaries. But her care was not limited to those like her in near or distant lands. From 1947 to 1967 Rosalie served as the director of the International Christian Conference for Negro Women at Benedict College. This summer institute trained hundreds for Christian service.

Rosalie's passion for interracial ministry was kindled by the experience of trying to find help for a maid whom she loved. One day the maid became ill, and Rosalie drove her to see the town doctor. Along the way the illness of the maid required her to seek a rest room. Again and again Rosalie stopped to ask assistance, but none of the businesses would allow the needy black woman to use their facilities. From that point on Rosalie knew her mission for Christ was as close as her own community.

Rosalie worked for racial justice in the Deep South before and through the civil rights movement because she believed the gospel should know no social barriers. For her efforts Rosalie was often ostracized in area churches and she can still remember the disdainful murmurs that rose when she entered the restaurants of her community.

As Rosalie has aged, her activities have necessarily been curtailed, but not her zeal for God's work. Rosalie taught a Sunday school class in her church for forty years and she is not about to let her knowledge waste away. To this day Rosalie spends every Saturday with her housekeeper, Bennie, ministering in another way. With Rosalie's books spread about them, Bennie and Rosalie sit together in Rosalie's home preparing for the class Bennie will teach in her church the next day. Rosalie shares forty years of lesson plans and works through her Bible study helps with Bennie. The knowledge and commitments of a lifetime keep rippling through more lives because of the love of Rosalie Cassels for the Lord and his people.

Rosalie Cassels's life epitomizes for me what the third portion of this book addresses. When partnerships reflect the priorities of Christ, they have an impact on many other lives. Rosalie's parents committed themselves to the care of the poor in the establishment of a church. That church then taught others—including their daughter—to share the love of Jesus with others. When Rosalie took that love into a marriage with a man who was also committed to her and the Lord's work, then the love of Christ spread even farther through church, missionary, and societal reform activities. Today, as I write of Rosalie, that love still spreads from her home in South Carolina to every reader of this book wherever you may be.

In Rosalie's life we can see how parents' love affects children, who become parents, who pass the love to more families and to distant lands and to different people and to a broken society. Each loving union becomes part of the fabric of human relationships that God uses to weave his love into the lives of others. The next chapters explore these dynamics, showing how the love we share extends to and through others to fulfill God's purposes.

seven

Each for the Other as Parents

was staying in the home of a pastor—a man well known for the scholarship of his ministry and the significance of his church. As one of the guest speakers at the multiday conference hosted by this church, I spent the afternoons working on the evening messages. The pastor invited me to use the office in his home for these preparations. One afternoon while working there, I could not help overhearing the sounds of children playing outside the window. At least "playing" was one way of characterizing the activity. One child, the nine-year-old son of the pastor, was dominating the others with cruelty, profanity, and intimidation.

The son's performance was hard to listen to and even harder to study through, so after a while I walked out of the office to take a break. The room opened at the bottom of a stairway. As I passed the stairs, a movement at the second-floor landing caught my eye. I glanced up to see the boy's mother watching him out a window overlooking the yard. She was virtually a silhouette against the window. The light against the dark outline of her body made her posture a poignant picture of obvious pain. With shoulders

129

drooped and head down, she flinched at the latest profanity from her son. Then she heard me too, and as she turned to face me, I realized she was crying.

From where I stood, the mother knew that I had heard her child and through her tears she said, "I don't know what's wrong with my son. His father doesn't know either. Somehow we have failed. Our son is only nine years old, and we have already failed. We just don't know what we should do."

The mother was obviously near despair. Yet, hidden in her words was an acknowledgment that still beaconed a biblical hope. The mother said, "*We* don't know what *we* should do." Though they were unsure what course of action they should take, this husband and wife still recognized an obligation rested on them. Despite their child's antics and the aching he was causing them, these parents acknowledged they still were responsible for their child's nurture.

This is the essence of biblical parenting: not acquiescing to children's demands but seeking to provide for their need to live as God requires. Sometimes this parental service is pleasant and other times painful but it is always characterized by the selfless application of one's resources, insights, and energies to help a child grow in the knowledge and likeness of Christ. All aspects of biblical parenting—including training, encouragement, and discipline—seek to serve these spiritual interests of the child rather than the convenience, preference, or interests of the parent.

Selfless parenting requires fathers and mothers to pour *themselves* into the welfare of their children. Parents who raise children according to God's standards do not pass the primary responsibility for their children to other adults; they do not pass the responsibility to other institutions; they do not pass the responsibility to the child; they do not take a pass on the responsibility. Assuming the responsibility for the nurture of one's children is a personal duty to God and it cannot be passively fulfilled. Parents obedient to Scripture actively submit themselves to God in nurturing their children as his Word directs.

The key New Testament passage telling parents how to raise their children God's way follows the apostle Paul's discussion of the relationships of husbands and wives. Here the apostle puts the responsibility for child rearing squarely on parents:

Children, obey your parents in the Lord, for this is right. "Honor your father and mother"—which is the first commandment with a promise—"that it may go well with you and that you may enjoy long life on the earth." Fathers, do not exasperate your children; instead, bring them up in the training and instruction of the Lord.

Ephesians 6:1–4

As simple as these words appear, mothers and fathers in the decadent culture of that ancient time may have been tempted to a bit of exasperation with Paul. The words of instruction are so few! Only one sentence actually gives any direct instruction to parents. And, as a further complication, this sentence is addressed only to fathers.

Surely parents in that Roman world were not unlike us in wanting a healthy selection of child rearing manuals at their ancient equivalent of a bookstore at the mall. How could anyone in that age of rampant ungodliness raise children properly with so little guidance? Parents who have to raise children in this age will ask the same question. With all the cultural perils facing our children, and with all the consequent questions facing us, does the Bible sufficiently equip parents? We cannot answer yes unless we consider the building blocks undergirding a child's nurture that the apostle laid prior to framing these few words of parental instruction. The Bible's short instruction to parents follows a host of instructions for the household of faith. This structure should remind us that God has clear expectations for the relationships that form the context and foundation of biblical child rearing. In outlining these relationships and their accompanying responsibilities, the Lord gives parents much guidance for rearing children in his care.

A Love Relationship with the Lord— The First Building Block

Paul's instruction to parents grows out of a larger discussion of how the church should operate. This earlier foundation is not

131

inconsequential. It means the Lord expects biblical parenting to occur in a church context. We can learn much about parenting from those in the church—through the preaching of the Word, the example of elders, and the advice of other Christian parents. Especially when my wife and I were first-time parents, we took many cues about raising our child from other couples in the church whose families we respected.

Beyond these practical implications, however, there is a more fundamental reason why the Bible teaches parenting in a church context. God's true church is made up of those whose hearts are committed to Christ (Eph. 3:16–21). The formal relationship one has with a church should be indicative of one's personal relationship with God. This means that a deep, personal relationship with the Lord is the most basic building block of Christian parenting. A Christian parent's first priority and most important duty is to love Jesus.

To more fully sense the importance of the tie between God's love and good parenting, consider how Paul begins his instruction to Christian households: "Be imitators of God, therefore, as dearly loved *children* and live a life of love, just as Christ loved us and gave himself up for us" (Eph. 5:1–2, italics mine). We learn how to love others by understanding how God loves us as his children. His love for us becomes the pattern for the way we love. In this way our own children become the most direct beneficiaries of our deep, personal understanding of God's parental care.

To prepare for our own parental care, Paul expresses God's love in parental terms over and over in his letter. Even his opening greeting stresses God's parental love:

> Grace and peace to you from God our *Father* and the Lord Jesus Christ. Praise be to the God and *Father* of our Lord Jesus Christ, who has blessed us in the heavenly realms with every spiritual blessing in Christ. For he chose us in him before the creation of the world to be holy and blameless in his sight. In love he predestined us to be *adopted* as his *sons* through Jesus Christ, in accordance with his pleasure and will.
>
> Ephesians 1:2–5, italics mine

These loving words demonstrate Paul's zeal to root our parental practices in a solid understanding of our relationship with our heavenly Father. There are at least two reasons that a love relationship with God is a necessary foundation stone for biblical parenting. The first relates to parents' need for a *model,* and the second to our need for *security.*

Our Heavenly Model

We tend to become our parents. For good or ill, parental models significantly shape us. Abusers raise abusers, alcoholics raise alcoholics, well-adjusted parents raise well-adjusted children. Of course there is comfort in this equation only if you are on the positive side. Fear and despair press in, however, if you recognize your own parents' modeling was inadequate or horrid. How can we hope to raise our children well if our own models are broken? The words of the apostle rescue *Christian* parents raised in deprived situations from hopelessness by reminding them that they are on the positive side of the child-development equation.

The Father of all Christians is God. The passage quoted above says simply that God is "our Father." The obvious grace in this simple statement is more profound to some of us than others. The truth that God is our Father frees us from our past. Because we have a heavenly parent, we are not bound to the negative patterns and practices of our earthly parents. We are not destined to repeat their errors because theirs is not the only imprint on us. God provides us with another parental model as well— himself.

The reality of the heavenly Father's love can be more real, more powerful, more motivating than biology and learned behavior. For this reason an intimate relationship with him does more to establish what we will be as parents than any other single factor in our existence or background. The realization that *the Father we perceive our God to be largely shapes the parent we are able to be* challenges us to make sure that our understanding of, and consequent relationship with, our God is biblical.

Our Heavenly Security

When the apostle says that God has been a Father to us since before the creation of the world, Paul directly reinforces the security we must have to be effective Christian parents (Eph. 1:4–5). Our greatest failings as parents typically result from our insecurities. I recognize this in myself when I confess what usually upsets me most with my children. What makes me angriest? Too often it is what my children do that embarrasses me or makes me look bad. In such moments I find that I can easily discipline out of my concern for me rather than out of a primary concern for my children's welfare. At its root such selfish discipline is a fear of the rejection of people outside my family. Buried beneath my anger is the fear that others will not think as highly of me as I desire—that I will be relegated to the sidelines of their acceptance or respect.

Conversely, I recognize it is often difficult for my wife (and for many other women) to discipline because of the fear that a child will be upset with her or reject her. Fear of a child's getting angry, turning a cold shoulder, or spurning a mother's love has stifled many a mom's discipline—and stirred many a child's rebellion.

Of course these are not gender-specific traits. There are plenty of fathers who will not discipline for fear of a child's rejection and many mothers who serve their own egos through managing the performance of their children. My point is not that both mothers and fathers have flaws but that insecurity can affect the behavior of us all. If we are more concerned about how people outside the family view us, we tend to overreact in discipline. If we are more concerned about how those within the family view us, we tend to underreact in discipline.

The sum of these truths is that anxious parents do not make good parents. So the Bible deals with the source of our anxieties by assuring Christian parents that God dearly loves us and has so loved us since before the creation of the world. Once this assurance takes deep root in a mother's or father's heart, it helps minimize the concern for protecting self that can be the hidden but driving motive behind our parenting decisions. Our security in our relationship with God frees us to parent for our children's good rather than for our own—giving to them our security rather than taking it from them (see Eph. 5:2).

A Love Relationship with a Spouse—
The Second Building Block

The necessity of parenting from personal security further explains why Paul talks about the relationship between spouses before discussing parenting (Eph. 5:22–33). He is concerned for more than biological order. His words establish a relational priority that grounds biblical parenting. My relationship with my wife should so confirm her personal security with the Lord that she can afford to do what is best for our children, even if that action threatens a child's acceptance of her. My wife's relationship with me should be such a reinforcement of my own security with the Lord that I do not need to discipline my children for my ego's sake. A healthy relationship between husband and wife provides the spiritual support that grounds discipline in love for the child rather than concern for the parent. God pours his love for children through parents whose priorities have developed within a context of personal confidence and security. Thus a second building block for a child's nurture is the love the parents share for each other.

The Bible says much about how husbands and wives should love before saying a little about how they should parent (Eph. 5:22–33). The implicit message is that a healthy relationship between a husband and wife is a prerequisite for biblical parenting. This does not mean that single parents cannot do a good job of raising children, when, through the providence of God, they have sole charge, but this is not the regular pattern of Scripture. The reasons that God desires tightly bonded parents are more than the pragmatics of having a united front when it comes to discipline (though such shoulder-to-shoulder responses are an important indication to a child of parental unity). More important is what that unity itself should accomplish.

Teaching Commitment

Through the completing of a man and a woman that a healthy marriage nurtures, a child learns a healthy pattern of intimacy, not just with another person but with God. What, after all, is the ultimate goal of the submission of a wife to her husband's authority and the sacrifice of the husband's prerogatives to the needs of his wife? The ultimate aim is to bring the reality of Christ's love into the marriage. To the extent that parents enable each other to learn and love Christ more, they also establish the model of intimacy that ultimately teaches the child what intimacy with the Lord means. Expressions of love for one another in the home are a direct path to understanding God's love for each of us. As a result, it is important to resurrect the time-tested and biblically corroborated truth that the greatest earthly gift you can give your child is a loving relationship with your spouse.

Nothing more clearly indicates to me the impact of the parents' marriage on a child's nurture than the family history of a Christian brother who shared his life's story with me. He was raised in a large family with siblings whose ages are widely separated. He reports that a line of spiritual and emotional health seems to be drawn in the sand of time separating those children raised in the early, healthy years of his parents' marriage and those raised when his parents' relationship was deteriorating. Emotional health, solid marriages, and spiritual maturity characterize the now-adult, older children. Conversely, troubled psyches, brushes with the law, and spiritual indifference mark the younger children. No one can prove a direct cause and effect for the differences in these siblings. Healthy marriages do not ensure well-adjusted children, and healthy children sometimes emerge from the most unhealthy home environments. Still, Scripture affirms what our own experience and instincts indicate: Healthy marriages typically are the soil from which healthy children spring.

This conclusion is not merely anecdotal. In a recent sampling of students at a prestigious university, almost half cited their parents' divorce as their "most determinative life-changing event."[1] The stories and statistics of these future leaders join with Scripture to testify that safeguarding the parents' marriage relationship remains an essential element of a child's nurture.

Because the relationship between parents is a primary conduit of God's grace into a family, a parent who slights his or her spouse for career advancement, unnecessary economic advantage, or even ministry concerns ultimately hurts the child. The eternal consequences of selfish advancements bought at the expense of a healthy home cannot be underestimated. Not even the pursuit of ministry at the expense of a family will serve God's purposes, since ministries are destroyed by broken families.

For the good of a child, the love of one's spouse must even take precedence over the relationship of the parent with that child. A parent who pours affection and attention into children at the expense of honoring a spouse may seem to be serving the children, but such priorities actually jeopardize the ultimate welfare of children. Because God intends for the parents' relationship to bring the reality of Christ's love into the home, a spouse who sacrifices the marriage—even out of apparent concern for the child—jeopardizes the spiritual welfare of that child. When the parents' love for each other takes a backseat to any earthly concern—even a child—the child's ability to know the character of the heavenly Father is hampered.

By these standards the Bible does not encourage parents to slight their children for their own selfish pursuits and enjoyments. Parents are simply not permitted to neglect each other by directing the love that God intends for their spouse to their child.

A loving relationship with God and a loving relationship with a spouse form the foundation of biblical parenting. When we assume the responsibilities of biblical parenting, we subject ourselves to the consequences of these truths. This means we commit ourselves to honoring God and our spouse for the sake of children even when such commitments prove to be trying and difficult.

Giving Comfort

Understanding that parenting grows out of more foundational relationships can give us important comfort. The Bible's emphases show that the daily context of Christian living is the most powerful tool of child rearing, rather than a precise set of right or wrong parental behaviors. A child's nurture is not determined by a list of rules that we mysteriously divine from Scripture's relatively few statements on specific parenting practices. This conclusion flies in the face of some handbooks on Christian parenting that teach there is only one correct way to affirm or show affection or discipline. Some have even claimed biblical proof for the proper feeding times of infants. Such instructions defy the liberties of Scripture and deny the dignity of individual differences. This kind of teaching also seems to imply that children are likely to be ruined if we make a single mistake in some particular moment or aspect of a child's upbringing. This is precisely what Scripture does *not* attest.

We will all make mistakes as parents. This does not automatically make us bad parents nor immediately threaten the ultimate welfare of our children. There are actions and practices through which I know my wife and I have made mistakes with our children. There have been times of improper discipline, impatience, and poor judgment that I hope their young minds will not recall. Still, Scripture does not require me to believe that a momentary error will wreck my children. Were I to believe it could, then I would become paralyzed for fear of doing something that would forever ruin them; or I might refuse ever to examine my parenting patterns lest I have to confess that I had warped my children by past mistakes. Because God places the foundations for biblical child rearing in a spiritual- and marital-relationship context, no single act of well-intentioned parenting is determinative of a child's future. The grace that a Christian heart embraces and that a Christian's marriage should foster allows Christian parents the privilege to fail, to seek forgiveness, and to try again. The Father's unconditional, eternal love erases the dread that a momentary lapse or a mistake in judgment will ruin our children or destroy our own relationship with him. This grace of God frees Christians to parent without second-guessing every act of discipline or feeling the need to deny past errors.

The Responsibilities of the Child—
The Third Building Block

The fact that we can make mistakes and still be good parents does *not* mean that God, therefore, releases us from the responsibility of conscientiously promoting godly character in our children. The Bible not only reveals the relationships that form the foundation of Christian parenting; God's Word also describes the responsibilities that should direct the actions of both parents and children.

We will parent well only if we know what God wants to nurture in our children. What does God expect children to do? The simple answer is that he expects them to obey (Eph. 6:1).

Special qualifications accompany the obedience God requires of children. The Bible tells children to submit to their parents "in the Lord." This means that a child should do whatever parents require so long as their instruction is not contrary to God's will or Word. However, Scripture also makes it clear that this submission is to be more than just *doing* what a parent requires. Sullen, angry, begrudging fulfillment of duty is not acceptable. An obedient child must also *honor* father and mother (Eph. 6:2). Children must submit in action and attitude to their parents' instruction.

Submission Is Right

The apostle Paul supplies two reasons for such submission. First, children are to obey "for this is right" (Eph. 6:1). What a peculiarly simple and, at first glance, unnecessary statement. Despite our temptation to retort, "Of course," there is great wisdom in the apostle's simple affirmation of the rightness of a child's obedience. We sense the importance of his remark when we wonder whether to make our children obey. Consider that moment when a little, three-year-old bundle of sugar and spice, bedecked in the finery of a new Easter dress, ignores her daddy's no and grabs a handful of candy from the table treats intended for guests. Then, when Daddy patiently tells this precious package of lace and sweetness to put the candy back, she says, "No." Now Daddy knows that if he does anything about this rebellion, he will feel like the grinch who stole Easter. What should this father require? What does the Bible say? Children, obey your parents *for this is right.*

Because God knows that we parents are easily torn by our love for our children and our insecurities about ourselves, he graciously speaks plainly. When our hearts wrestle with the question, Should I insist my child obey? God answers, Yes, "for this is right." When a young mother cannot bring herself to discipline her child, when a father will not provide the time or attention to discipline, when the latest child rearing book has made you question whether you should just ignore some improper outburst from your child—in each of these moments we need the straightforward simplicity this Scripture supplies.

Of course there are moments when our circumstances, or our children's situations, will require discretion regarding the timing and degree of our disciplinary measures. Still, we cannot make dismissal of discipline a pattern. If we think we love our children too much to require them to do what is right, then we have not really loved them enough.

Submission Is Good

The apostle explains why there is a relationship between loving our children and disciplining them when he gives the second reason for children to submit to their parents. Not only is it right for our children to obey, it is good for them (Eph. 6:2–3). God promises obedient children *blessing* ("that it may go well with you") and *safekeeping* ("that you may enjoy long life on earth"). This last statement does not guarantee that obedience will ward off all disease and accidents. It is rather a repetition of the general promise of well-being that accompanies the fifth of the Ten Commandments, telling children to obey. (Note, however, that the promise also has a literal fulfillment in that children who honor God with their lives will be kept safe for eternity on this earth when it is renewed by Christ's return.) In effect, the apostle warns that a disobedient child endangers himself physically and spiritually.

The dangers of disobedience were well demonstrated to my family on a long-ago trip to an amusement park. We were waiting in line for a train ride. As the wait lengthened, a five- or six-year-old child in front of us decided to climb on a fence railing to a position that made it hard for the remaining people in line to pass. His mother reacted quickly, saying, "Johnny, come down from there." Johnny did not move even an eyelash.

A litany of parental attempts at correction soon followed. Had the damage being done to the child's character by these attempts not been so evident, these words would have been comical:

"Johnny, come down from there, right now!

"Johnny, come down. I won't tell you again.

"Johnny, I am going to count to three. One, two, . . . two and a half. . . . Now, Johnny, I mean it.

"Johnny, I am going to tell your father when we get home.

"Okay, Johnny, just stay there. I'm going to leave you if you don't come down.

"Johnny, please, please come down. I'll buy you an ice-cream cone."

We squeezed by the child when it was our turn to ride the train, but for all we know Johnny is now twenty years old and still sitting on that fence rail.

If you can re-create that incident in your mind's eye, think not only of the stone-cold look on Johnny's face. Consider the countenance of the surrounding people. What do their faces reflect? They are all frowning at the child. Responsible parents must dare to look at these faces because they prophesy the future of an uncontrolled child. A child who will not obey a parent's authority will see only the world's frown.

Not only does such an undisciplined child inherit a parent's frustration, he also reaps the disapproval of teachers, neighbors, other parents, friends, future employers, and ultimately his own heart. A child who consistently sees his reflection in the frown of the world can view himself only as despised. This is why the Book of Proverbs says that parents who will not discipline, hate their child (13:24). Such parenting subjects a child to a lifetime of misery—a fate we typically desire only for our enemies.

141

A disobedient child is a bother to the world and also a danger to himself. Only a few days ago in a nearby park I witnessed a child racing away from a father, who was frantically calling, "Jason, don't run that way!"

"Why, Daddy?" asked Jason as he kept running, soon tumbling headlong over a hill into a concrete culvert.

The child's bloodied forehead was a painful corroboration and a vivid object lesson of this Scripture's truth. We raise obedient children because this is right for them and it is good for them. Godly obedience protects children from the consequences of disobedience that are both earthly and eternal, for, ultimately, a child who does not know obedience cannot know the Lord.

The Responsibilities of the Parent— The Fourth Building Block

The final building block in the foundation of child rearing is formed from the expectations God has for parental obedience. Simply stated, *parents* are to raise their children. The Bible's words carry an implicit understanding of who is to do the raising of a child. Fathers and mothers are those given parenting instructions (Eph. 6:2–4), not grandparents, not paid baby-sitters or servants, not institutions outside the home. This does not mean the Bible forbids parents ever to utilize the services of others in fulfilling the biblical responsibilities of child care. Still, the words of Scripture challenge all parents to make sure they are the *chief* caregivers.

We must be especially careful in our society because social, economic, and spiritual pressures are tearing parents from their home responsibilities, and this imperils our families. Too many parents have virtually turned over the upbringing of their children to day care, school care, church care, grandparents, or nannies. Economic necessities or family exigencies too numerous to list here may well force parents to handle their children's care in a number of ways they may not prefer. Life is not always served to us in *Leave It to Beaver* packages. But where our children's future is involved, we must take great care to examine whether genuine necessity justifies the time our children spend away from our care.

I want to emphasize here that no one unfamiliar with the specific complexities facing your family has a right to determine that you are automatically sinning by using any version or amount of these nonparental care systems. The question of who is raising your child is determined by the degree of conscientious, committed involvement you invest in your child's nurture. It is not a matter of putting a stopwatch on the hours a child spends here or there. Nevertheless, a husband and wife working long hours in demanding jobs that leave them both exhausted at the end of the day when they pick up kids from Grandma's or day care must question whether they are submitting themselves to the family model the Bible intends. Bigger homes, nicer cars, and longer vacations, purchased at the price of absent parents, cost the family far too much and may well indicate the parents' submission to values that are distant from those taught in Scripture.

The fact that the parenting God requires is a spiritual discipline helps explain the wording the apostle Paul uses to instruct parents. Paul addresses "fathers" with his only specific instruction for child rearing (Eph. 6:4). This is not because the apostle thinks mothers have no role in child rearing. He clearly identifies the mother's importance when he instructs children to "honor your father and mother" (6:2). However, by addressing the spiritual head of the home directly, the apostle underscores the spiritual challenge and significance of biblical parenting. Because the Bible holds the spiritual head of the home accountable for the nurture of children, the task has obvious spiritual priority. While a man may need to delegate child rearing responsibilities, he cannot turn over all child rearing decisions and activities to another. A father remains biblically responsible for the nurture of his children.

In the writings of the apostle Paul, *father* most often refers to God in his relationship with believers. This word echo should help men understand that we are to nurture our children in the way that God fathers us. He never fails to guard our well-being and he offers willingly his presence and care to nurture us.

Such fathering is in shamefully short supply in our society no matter where we look. Television news specials have recently shifted the blame for our nation's inner-city problems from drugs to the absence of fathers in urban homes. But the fathering crisis is not limited to the poor neighborhoods of our nation's cities. In that same sampling of students at the leading university already cited, only one of these best and brightest of America's children mentioned a father when asked to list the factors that contributed most in molding their lives.[2] At all rungs of our society fathers have led the parental abdication of family responsibilities.[3] The Bible leads parents back into homes through the headship of fathers. Scripture's specific words and family perspective remind us that parenting is a high spiritual priority that both mother and father must take care not to slight.

Having laid the foundation of relationships and responsibilities on which God expects us to build our parenting, the apostle next issues his instructions for Christian parents through the comments he directs to fathers (Eph. 6:4). Through these imperatives God tells us how his expectations for our children should translate into parental action. These divine commands to which Christian parents must submit themselves come in both negative and positive form—we are told what not to do, and then what to do.

What Parents Should *Not* Do— The Fifth Building Block

Submitting ourselves to our children's welfare means first that Christians must *not* parent with unbiblical patterns or priorities. The Bible says, "Do not exasperate your children" (Eph. 6:4). Understanding the special term Scripture uses for this negative instruction unfolds its broad implications for parenting. The Old Testament usage of *exasperate* (in the Greek translation with which Paul would have been familiar) does not simply refer to frustration, anger, or anxiety. The term describes God's own just anger over Israel's idolatry. The exasperation described here refers to a righteous resentment of actions or attitudes inconsistent with one's faith commitments. Thus an exasperated child is one who has a right to be provoked because of the inconsistencies between a parent's stated beliefs and that parent's actual behaviors.

Our children have a right to be upset with us when our parental actions conflict with our spiritual values. We do not have to guess what values the apostle has in mind in this passage of the Bible. Preceding verses stress the importance of using authority based on the example of Christ, expressing love patterned after the sacrifice of Christ, and showing respect out of reverence for Christ. What would be inconsistent with these values that would cause exasperation in children?

> *Authority that requires submission but submits to none,* as when a mother tells a child to quit whining by whining at him, or when a father compels self-control by throwing a temper tantrum.
>
> *Love that requires sacrifice but seeks self,* as when a mother pushes for a child's success to affirm her own worth, or when a father punishes to enforce behavior that secures reputation, adulation, or service for himself.
>
> *Respect demanded at the expense of individual dignity,* as when a mother shames a child into obedience, or when a father exerts control by comparing the child with others inside or outside the family.

Whether discipline takes the form of manipulative guilt trips, shaming silent treatments, or abusive denials of a child's worth, the home that rules by condemnation undermines biblical obedience. The essence of biblical parenting is recognizing that we are the dispensers of God's grace into our children's lives. Our children learn to identify and reverence God's character through the way we treat them, both in moments of profound pride and in times of intense disappointment.

When one of my children was younger I struggled to apply these truths. My son bordered on being hyperactive and was always on the edge of being out of control. I was unprepared to deal with a child who seemed not only unconcerned about his own safety but also appeared to be unaware of what behavior various social contexts required. His antics consistently endangered him and embarrassed us.

We used lots of traditional discipline—methods that worked with our other children—to try to coerce this son's obedience. I sometimes found myself spanking him three, four, or more times a day attempting to gain control of him, but to my dismay my efforts failed.

No amount of correction changed this child. His constant misconduct began to frustrate and demoralize the whole family. As a result, I found I was sometimes disciplining out of the fury I felt over my own failure. With my anger, resentment also began to grow between my son and me. His behavior challenged my own sense of parental adequacy. Even worse, he began to think of himself as a "wild" child because I had begun to talk about him that way. My concern for my own reputation and authority were robbing my son of my love, his dignity, and God's grace.

Something had to change. One day I said to my wife, "I can't spank him anymore." This was as much an admission of my failure as it was a decision to try something else. Stubborn adherence to discipline measures that had worked with my other children, that were part of my own background, and that demanded the least change in me had, in fact, driven me from what I knew Christian parenting required. I felt I was damaging my son to prove my parental competence.

We began to consider alternative ways of compelling our son's obedience because we knew abandoning discipline was not biblically permissible. God was gracious. First, he brought into my wife's choir a child development expert who told us that in their developing years brilliant children (such as our son) are often hyperactive, not out of intentional disobedience, but out of their brains' constant demands for new sources of information and stimuli. This insight helped us understand our son. Second, the Lord helped us recall that even in our child's most excitable moments, he would almost always settle down when his mother took him into her lap, stroked his hair, and told him about how thrilled we were the day God brought him into our world. If we could just capture the dynamics of that calming mechanism, we thought we might have a new discipline tool.

For the next several months whenever control was needed, instead of spanking, we simply made our son sit down wherever he was. He had to stop and be still until we said he could resume his activity. For this active child such time-outs were almost torture, but we insisted. The technique did *not* work like a charm, but over a period of weeks, we began to see results. By our allowing him to decompress, instead of overloading his system with the additional stimulation of a spanking, our son was able to gain more control of himself.

In hindsight I feel foolish when I consider the mistakes I made with my son. Yet confession of these errors gives me a greater appreciation for the wisdom of Scripture and more understanding of God's grace. By insisting that a child respond to a single kind of discipline in the same manner as his siblings, I was not allowing my son the dignity of being the individual God made him. The Lord has developed my son into a special person. I am very proud of the spiritual maturity and knowledge evident in his life. Yet, I recognize that I could have greatly damaged these evidences of God's grace in my son if the Lord had not made my errors apparent. By not separating discipline for my child's welfare from concern about my own reputation and authority, I was allowing selfishness to motivate my parenting.

Godly parenting should reflect a deep understanding of our Lord's grace. Out of respect for the individual gifts God has granted my children, I must submit myself to the responsibility of discovering ways to discipline them that honor the unique ways God has made them and plans to use them. Biblical parenting requires me to respect the dignity of my children's differences, to use my authority selflessly, and to affirm their worth without seeking to inflate mine. As my children have grown older and as their maturing involves issues more complex and prolonged than in earlier years, I have discovered how important it is simply to resolve to love them—and to express my resolve even when we differ. In short, more and more I realize that my parenting must remain consistent with my understanding of the grace God extends to me. I must not exasperate my children by disciplining for my sake (rather than theirs) and without regard for the unique ways God has made and is maturing each of them.

147

What Parents Should Do—
The Sixth Building Block

God does not tell us merely *what not to do* for our children's welfare. Thankfully he tells us *what to do* as well. Scripture instructs Christian parents to "bring them [children] up in the training and instruction of the Lord" (Eph. 6:4). The great theologian John Calvin communicated the import of this "bring them up" phrase, by translating the words as, "let them [children] be fondly cherished." This interpretation reflects how the Bible uses these nurturing terms elsewhere. The apostle Paul uses a similar kind of wording earlier in this passage when saying a husband should cherish his wife as much as he "cares" for his own body and just as Christ does the church (5:29). Paul now intensifies these concepts in his instruction to fathers regarding the care of their children. The effect of this wording is that the apostle tells each father to care for his child as deeply and intensely as possible—as much as he "cares" for his own flesh.

The biblical use of these terms has deep theological significance for parenting. As the first husband, Adam, "cared" for his wife as flesh of his flesh (i.e., the product of his own body); and as Christ "cares" for his bride, the church (which is the product of his sacrificed flesh), so we as parents are to "care" intensely for our children. They are the product of our flesh. Since our life is in them, we are to bring up our children with the care we give to our own bodies. We should nurture our children as the essence of our lives. This means the physical and spiritual vitality God grants Christians should also thrive in their children as the product of sacrificial care. Parents are to be givers, pouring themselves into the nurture of those God commits to their keeping.

How do we nurture with such care? The apostle Paul gives two words to guide: "training" and "instruction." Both of these terms refer to the discipline of children but with slightly different shades of meaning. *Training* carries the more positive connotation—parents are to model, teach, and encourage godly patterns of life. *Instruction* contains a slightly negative nuance—parents are to warn, correct, and discipline when actions or attitudes are inconsistent with godliness. The shades of meaning may be a bit more clear in older translations that encourage parents to raise children "in the *nurture* and *admonition* of the Lord." The biblical writers most typically use these words when describing the ways Scripture itself instructs believers through caring guidance and loving reproof. Paul's use of the same terms should remind us that godly parenting requires a balance of affirmation and correction.

The scriptural instruction to provide a balance of firm guidance and loving correction finds almost startling corroboration in modern family research:

Delinquents and criminals tend to come from homes in which discipline is *overstrict or erratic,* supervision is unsuitable, neither parent shows warmth or love, and there is little or no closeness of family members. Nondelinquents are more apt to come from homes in which discipline is *firm but kindly,* supervision is suitable, parents show affection for the child, and the family does many things together [italics mine]. . . . Research in the area of child development shows that "firm but kindly" is optimal. Diana Baunrind (1970), in a ten year study of parent-child relationships, found that *authoritative* parenting in which the parent exerts firm control without hemming the child in with too many restrictions is more apt to produce a motivated, friendly, moral, and cooperative child than either *authoritarian* parenting in which the parent attempts to shape, control, and evaluate all the activities of the child, or *permissive* parenting in which few demands are placed upon the child who is permitted to do whatever he or she pleases. . . . The children of authoritarian parents tend to be discontented, distrustful, and lacking in warmth, while the children of permissive parents tend to be the least self-reliant and self-controlling of all three groups. Children reared permissively are often said to be spoiled and may become tyrants who rule over their own parents. . . .

Authoritative parents use a unique combination of high control and positive encouragement of the child's autonomy and independence. There is no question but that the parent is in charge. Guidelines and rules are given within which the child must operate, and standards for future conduct are set. But parents share their reasons for the rules and encourage verbal give-and-take on the part of the child. Both the rights and interests of the parents and the rights and interests of the child are taken into consideration.[4]

How do we achieve this balance of training and instruction, of affirmation and correction, of firm but kindly parenting? The answer lies in the final words of the apostle Paul's instruction. We are to raise our children in the training and instruction "of the Lord." The chief goal of parenting is to enable children to know and honor God. This means we parents should constantly examine whether our words, our manner, our correction, and our home environment nurture an understanding of the Lord. This requires more than the application of a specific technique of discipline or setting a curfew in accord with the standards of the latest parenting seminar.

No single set of techniques or rules will make us good parents. Our sins and our children are far more perplexing than any book, seminar, or sermon can comprehensively cover. I am *not* devaluing the many helpful things that we can learn from Christian authors and other experienced parents. We simply must remember that the complexities of each child's nature and situations will not allow template responses.

This uniqueness of each child should not frustrate or bewilder us. Rather we can take it as a biological affirmation of the beautiful creativity God has applied to making each of our children special. Not only does the uniqueness of each child affirm his or her individual dignity, it has the additional benefit of driving each conscientious Christian parent back to the foundation of Christian living—the prudent application of scriptural principles discerned by a heart in tune with the Lord. A loving relationship with God is fundamental to Christian parenting. This is especially obvious when we are talking about discipline. For if we do not have a grip on grace, then we will not have the courage to discipline; but if grace has no grip on us, then there will be no constraint on our discipline.

Parenting by Grace

Christian parenting compels us to reflect our God and as a consequence leads us to greater dependence on him and to a greater appreciation of him. By submitting ourselves to the good of children, we discover our own most noble purposes and are drawn most closely to the divine nature. News reports of the actions of two parents aboard Amtrak's Sunset Limited in 1993 revealed these truths with a powerful poignancy.

Gary and Mary Jane Chancey were riding on the Limited on a foggy September morning when the train plunged off a railway bridge into a bayou outside Mobile, Alabama. The Chanceys were traveling with their eleven-year-old daughter, Andrea, who has cerebral palsy and requires a wheelchair. As their train car sank into the bayou, water rushed into the Chanceys' capsized compartment. Fighting the flow of water rushing through the window, the two parents combined their efforts to lift Andrea to a rescuer. Then the water pressure overwhelmed them, pushed them deep into the darkness of the train cabin, and they were gone.

These parents gave their lives to the purpose of lifting their child to physical safety. God calls all Christian parents to similar sacrifice, enduring what may be intense pressure and pain to lift our children to spiritual safety. We are not all called to die for our children, but we die to self each time—for our children's sake—we hold our tongues, control our anger, endure being misunderstood, take time for a ball game, absorb an insult, ignore an embarrassment, turn down a promotion requiring more time away, love patiently, discipline consistently, and forgive always. By the ways we love God and each other, by the ways we model the Lord and mold our children's perception of him, by the way we raise them in the patterns of his love, and by the way we constantly seek his direction—in all of these ways we give ourselves so that our children may understand their Savior's love for them. In doing so, we discern the love we require as well as the love we must give. By lifting our children to the Savior, we become like him and thus discover in a parent's heart another means to measure and to marvel at the love of the Savior who lifts us to heaven by his sacrifice.

eight

Each for the Other in Society

On December 12, 1985, a chartered commercial airliner carrying 248 servicemen from the 101st Army Airborne Division crashed while taking off from Gander, Newfoundland. Jeff Owens of Hockessin, Delaware, was not on the plane.

The day before, Jeff had cursed his luck as he watched his comrades leave without him to begin the long flight home from an assignment in the Sinai. Jeff had actually booked the seating for all the soldiers and had made sure to set aside seating for himself and his company commander. However, when the time came to file his own paperwork to reserve his seat, Jeff was on a sightseeing excursion in Egypt. He missed the filing deadline by only two hours. Pulling every string he knew as the executive officer of the company commander, Jeff still was not able to wrangle a seat on the plane that was to head home over the route that would require the brief stop in Newfoundland.

Because he had booked the seating for the soldiers, Jeff was the only one who knew who was actually on the plane. To him fell the task of reviewing his paperwork to confirm for his superiors and the world the names of each of the 248 soldiers who died. This was the largest peacetime loss of life that the Army had ever experienced, and Jeff's anger grew with the report of each additional name.

Though Jeff was not living as a Christian, he had grown up with a Christian mother and now he questioned how God could allow such a tragedy. Particularly galling to Jeff was the death of his company commander. The commander was Jeff's dear friend and had talked to Jeff about the beauty and joy of Christian faith. Says Jeff, "I was very angry at God for a very long time because he would let such a faithful man die so senselessly."

As news of the crash spread across the world, Jeff quickly called his mother to inform her that he had not been among those who crashed at Gander. He told her about the bizarre delays that had kept him from the flight despite his own attempts to get on the plane. She replied, "God must have had some reason to keep you off the plane." They were words that Jeff was not ready to hear but they would echo in his heart when he traveled to see the wife of his company commander.

A month after the crash in the wake of the Christmas season, Jeff asked hard questions of the young widow who was preparing to move from military housing at Fort Campbell. "Aren't you angry at God, since he took away your husband even though he was a Christian?" Jeff asked.

Jeff expected to hear regret, despair, rage, or at least frustration. Instead, the young woman reflected the faith that she and her husband had shared and reinforced in each other. She replied, "The Lord gave my husband a better Christmas present than I could ever have given him. He is with Jesus now."

They were words that did not entirely make sense to Jeff, but he left thinking to himself, "There is something real in her life that I do not have."

For the next four years, Jeff says, "I lived as if I was in control, but I knew, as I reflected on the 'chance' circumstances that had saved my life and as I considered the words of my mother and the widow of my commander, that God was leading me to a decision."

In 1989 Jeff visited his mother and "to make her happy" he went to church with her. In the Sunday school class there, he heard in clear terms of the God who leaves nothing to chance but works all things for an eternal purpose that is loving and good. Jeff realized that all his attempts to control his own life had failed. Despite his education, his military service, his job, his relationships—his life was not what he wanted and he felt he was increasingly losing control of it. Again he thought back to the time when he had tried to control his trip home from the Sinai only to see his efforts thwarted in a way that saved his life "for some reason." Jeff also remembered the confidence of the young widow who rejoiced in God's plans despite her loss. "Her words came to my mind and brought me to my knees," Jeff says. He committed his life to the one who was really in control for reasons that are beyond our knowledge but are for our eternal care.

This account reminds us that what happens in our homes has effects reaching far beyond our families. The faith that Jeff's company commander and his wife lived for each other reached beyond the walls of their home, beyond the life they shared together, and ultimately beyond this world through the eternal effects of their testimony. Not only did their commitments touch Jeff, but now as I write of the faith they shared, their testimony reaches to many more who read this book.

We cannot fully know how our lives ripple into other lives and eternities, but God assures us that he does not mean for us to restrict his love to our homes. The way we learn to live for each other in our most intimate relationships shapes our hearts and necessarily affects others by the way we treat them and live before them.

The apostle Paul demonstrates this when he unrolls the truths about how we should live sacrificially for each other beginning with husbands and wives, and then demonstrating how those principles would relate to other household relationships such as parents and children, then servants and masters. The apostle Peter not only moves beyond these household codes of conduct when discussing what it means for each to live for others, he also unwinds the principles from the other end—discussing general relationships before moving to intimate ones (1 Peter 2:13–3:9). Peter makes us consider what it means for each to live for the other in society and then he ties those truths to the home. In this way the Bible reminds us in an almost startling fashion that home life and outside life are intertwined. Each affects the other because both influence the character of the heart that must operate in all spheres of life.

What does it mean for each to live for the other outside the home? What does God require of you? Well-schooled Christians may think the answers to these questions come easily. In our childhoods we may have been taught a song incorporating these words from the prophet Micah: "What does the Lord require of you? To act justly and to love mercy and to walk humbly with your God" (Micah 6:8). The words come quickly to mind and roll readily off the tongue. In fact the requirements are so easy to state that we may not sense how important and difficult they are to fulfill. Peter assumes the obligation of letting us know just what these duties mean in real life when we face real people.

Duties to Others

The apostle's definition of our duty begins with details of the Christian's obligations to governing authorities. Peter says, "Submit yourselves for the Lord's sake to every authority instituted among men," whether the governance comes from the highest seat of power, such as a king, or from those to whom authority has been delegated (1 Peter 2:13–14). Whatever our estimation of the competence or character of the civil authorities in our culture, we as Christians must remember that a higher authority— God himself—arranged for our leaders' rule. For whatever purposes God has ordained, including challenging Christians to new levels of faithfulness to him, earthly rulers have authority (Rom. 13:1–2). This higher source of all human government places special obligations on Christians who would live sacrificially for God so that others will know his nature and character.

Higher Duty

Christians may not act as though they are above man's law. Though they owe ultimate allegiance to the laws of heaven, their testimony requires that they *submit to all authority* that does not require them to transgress God's law. The social structures that maintain the medium of human relationships necessary for the spread of the gospel as well as the testimony of Christians that validates the goodness of our message require us to honor the authority of those to whom God grants rule (1 Peter 2:14–15).

Most Christians will nod in ready agreement with this call to good citizenship until they think of the real-life implications. We are not allowed to excuse ourselves from submission to rulers simply because we do not like them, we find their standards inconvenient, they act unfairly, they are from a different political party, we disagree with their policies, or they support institutions abhorrent to God. As uncomfortable as this instruction may make us, its force is accentuated by the conditions under which Peter wrote. The apostle commanded his fellow Christians to submit to governing authorities when his own rulers were cruel pagans designing policies to persecute his fellow believers.

If Christians are ever tempted to dismiss Peter's words with the explanation, "That old apostle just does not understand the kinds of people who are in authority in our culture," then it is time for the reminder that the highest human authority when Peter wrote was Nero, the Roman ruler who fed Christians to lions.

Peter captures the reason for obedient regard for authorities when he says, "Submit yourselves *for the Lord's sake* to every authority instituted among men" (v. 13, italics mine). Our submission is for the sake of the Lord and not for the petty interests of earthly rulers. So long as the government maintains general order in society and does not require Christians to disobey God, then the truths about Jesus can spread through ordinary human relationships. Without order, this higher purpose of God and his people usually fails.

The events of our contemporary world testify to the power of God's higher purposes. Half a century ago a Communist government drove missionaries from China during the cultural revolution. At that time tens of thousands, perhaps as many as one or two million Christians, lived throughout all of China. In the intervening decades the atheistic government maintained the order of the vast population by frequent intimidation and inexpressible cruelties, yet Christianity spread from house to house. Now conservative estimates indicate there are between forty and sixty million Christians in China. By contrast, when governments fall apart (as in those Eastern European countries now embroiled in civil war), human relationships come unglued, and the spread of Christianity slows or even stops.

The higher purposes of God to inform people of eternal rescue from earthly trials are served when governments maintain order that keeps people tied together. For this reason Peter urges Christians to serve others in society by submitting to governing authorities—even those who by their own conduct deserve no honor. In this way more and more people may come to know Christ.

Peter further specifies the nature of Christian conduct in society by saying that we must *silence foolishness with righteousness* as part of our submission to authorities. The apostle says we must submit to governing authorities, "For it is God's will that by doing good you should silence the ignorant talk of foolish men" (v. 15). Peter wanted the exemplary conduct of believers to short-circuit rumors and accusations that Christians were troublesome zealots who could not function in Roman society because they would only honor their God. Nero, the ruler in Peter's day, displayed this foolish thinking when he blamed the burning of Rome on Christians—and he opened the door to the barbarous persecution of Christians as a result.

Christians today may well understand how difficult it is to resist foolish accusations with godly responses. Consider what labels are placed on you by the popular media, some politicians, and other "sophisticated" people if you identify yourself as a Bible-believing, evangelical Christian. You may see news reports that identify you as "intolerant," "bigoted," "illiterate," "angry," or even "violent." Neighbors may shy away from you as one who is "cultish," "fanatical," "fundamentalistic," or simply "crazy." You may know all of these labels are unfair, unkind, and untrue. You may be tempted to lash out with some labels of your own. But Peter says that you will better serve the Lord's purposes and the people who need to know him by "enduring" such foolishness and "doing good" in the midst of it.

In view of the foolish accusations of Christian lawlessness, the apostle urges believers not to use the rights they possess as disciples of the highest authority in the universe to excuse any wrongdoing on their part. "Live as free men," says Peter, "but do not use your freedom as a cover-up for evil" (v. 16). Though Christians serve the Lord and are not ultimately bound to man's laws, Peter says we must *live with integrity* before all. Even if others act immorally, unethically, or unfairly, Christians may not even the score by resorting to similar behaviors. Using unethical means to achieve a political victory, obtain a promotion, or even further the influence of a church does not please God. The wrongdoings of others never justify wrong actions by Christians whose testimony for God may be most powerful when they choose to lose rather than win at the world's games playing by the world's rules. We serve others' spiritual interests when we willingly suffer loss to show we trust God to make things right rather than engage in wrong to accomplish what we perceive is right.

The apostle underscores the degree of integrity he requires in the words that follow. He says that Christ's followers must "show proper respect to everyone" (v. 17). God's people do not fulfill their civil obligations when they merely offer outward conformity to the standards of those in power. The role Christians have in society's order requires them to approach all their relationships with proper attitudes as well as proper actions. Being phony will not spread the truth about Christ.

Showing proper respect does not mean that Christians approve evil or neglect speaking boldly about a leader's actions that dishonor God or disregard his Word. Still, to the extent that such individuals are made in the image of God and have authority allowed by God, we must treat them and their offices with proper dignity and honor (remember Peter wrote these words with Nero in mind). We do not offer this respect because our leaders are necessarily deserving of such honor, but because God intends for the godly attitudes and purposes of the Christian community to be apparent to all.

We should *love with sincerity* in all the contexts to which God calls us. God intends for the attitudes that are found within the Christian community to radiate outward, and this cannot be done authentically and powerfully if God's people are only pretending to care about others—or are only acting out of begrudging duty rather than out of the true desire to serve others. Thus to be true to God's purposes, Christians must "love the brotherhood of believers, fear God," and also "honor the king" (v. 17).[1] Attitudes must coincide with actions for God's purposes to prosper. The honor those in the church give to authorities ultimately reflects the respect Christians have for God, as well as the mutual regard for others that should characterize our fellowship.

When honor for leaders is absent, then it is very difficult to communicate the Christian love that God desires to demonstrate through his people. My family witnessed in an organization my children once attended how disrespect impedes the progress of the gospel. This Christian organization encouraged children to participate in community-building activities that would instill respect for our country and its people. Each meeting began with pledges of allegiance to the American flag and to the Christian flag. Further, as part of learning good citizenship, the children were encouraged to recite in order the names of all the American presidents. The kids actually got so good at their recitation that it began to bore them. So a few of the older boys began to spice up the opening ceremony by adding to the list of presidents a name that made the adults in attendance laugh.

After naming William Clinton as the forty-second president, the children added another name to the list of presidents—Hillary Clinton. The joke got such a good laugh that the children began to add the name every time they recited the list. The snorting chuckles of their adult supervisors did nothing to discourage the practice. Sadly what the adults did not recognize is what the disrespect encouraged.

In the name of Jesus Christ this "Christian" organization, whose purpose was to teach love for God and country, instead taught my children to hate. By not guarding attitudes as well as actions, this organization implicitly (if not explicitly) taught my children that it is okay to ridicule and demean someone with whom you disagree. My children learned that, though the Bible says to "show proper respect for everyone," what God really means is that we can make fun of our leaders and their families because we object to their policies. Thus by failing to honor our president as the Bible requires, this Christian organization promotes attitudes that will ultimately lead to the inability of its members to live by the Christian principles on which it claims to stand.

One of the most difficult tasks Christians in a democratic society face is boldly advocating God's purposes without abandoning God's principles. The gospel powerfully progresses when we speak truth in love, rather than matching insult for insult, and hate for hate (Eph. 4:15; 1 Peter 3:9). God calls us to such courageous compassion for the sake of Christ's purposes in our society and in our own hearts. By giving proper respect to everyone in society, we solidify the attitudes that give Christian foundation to our marriages, families, churches, and wider relationships.

Wider Duty

Having heard what the apostle Peter requires of Christians in regard to our relationships with authorities, we might wish that he would change channels. Instead, he turns up the volume by bringing the subject closer to home. Not only does the apostle say that we must show respect to distant governing authorities, he expands our obligations to include the daily authorities of our lives—those for whom we work.

Though Peter addresses "slaves" (1 Peter 2:18), we are wrong if we hear his words only in the context of the despicable, chattel slavery of American history. The word translated "slave" in this passage most naturally refers to household workers, which included those in apprentice or indentured relationships as well as captured enemies and lifelong servants. Some of these servants held positions of great responsibility in the ancient world, such as being city treasurers. Though the term applies to a great range of people in different occupations, still these workers ultimately depended for their livelihood on the approval and decisions of others. In this context Peter's instruction then and now most naturally applies to all who by reason of training, occupation, or situation have their lives controlled by another.

The spectrum of persons Peter was addressing makes it appropriate for those of us in modern employment situations to search for principles in the apostle's words that apply to how we relate to our bosses. This is not meant to minimize the misery of some of those Peter addressed. Having to *submit to your master* remains onerous in any age, and Peter himself reveals how awful such masters could be in his time (vv. 19–20). The terrible light in which this apostle places harsh masters is one of the ways the New Testament ultimately condemns chattel slavery without immediately outlawing all forms of servitude that were so much a part of the fabric of ancient society.

Peter begins his instruction to Christians who have masters (or employers) by using the now familiar terms of *submission* and *respect*. He says, "Submit yourselves to your masters with all respect" (v. 18). The terms necessarily broaden the Christian's obligations. We are obliged to deal respectfully, not only with political authorities but also with authorities in our place of work. Because these authorities are typically so much more involved in our daily lives than are political leaders, the apostle's words now have an immediacy and an intensity that the previous instruction may not have carried.

More pressure comes when Peter begins to characterize the people who sometimes serve as masters. While acknowledging that some are "good and considerate," Peter confesses some are "harsh" (v. 18). Thus Peter no longer merely orders us to endure foolishness, he now commands us to *endure injustice* for the sake of our testimony (vv. 19–20). The apostle is not simply talking figuratively. He gives no credit to servants who "receive a beating" for doing wrong, and by contrast commends those who endure unjust punishment for doing good.

The suffering that Peter has in mind is real and brutal, yet he wants us to remain "conscious of God" as we go through it. He explains how this consciousness affects our actions and attitudes in a further intensification of his earlier instruction. As citizens we are to live with integrity even when ruled by ungodly leaders. And as servants and employees we are to *live with Christ-likeness* even when we are abused. "To this [suffering for good] you were

called," says Peter, "because Christ suffered for you, leaving you
an example, that you should follow in his steps" (v. 21).

When we have been treated horridly by one who has control
of our livelihoods, no task seems more difficult than responding
with Christ-like attitudes and actions to our oppressor. The first
job I ever had outside my home made this truth abundantly clear
to me. The job allowed me to take advantage of my new driver's
license. I was put on a route to service candy-vending machines.
My job was to stock the machines, remove the money that had
accumulated over the past week, and split the proceeds with the
owner of the machines.

What the owner did not tell me was that his nephew had
worked the route before I did and had not turned in his keys to
the machines. After several days of not collecting nearly as much
money as my employer had promised when I took the job, I sus-
pected something was amiss. I discovered that the nephew was
preceding me on the route, using his keys to remove money from
the machines (leaving me to stock the machines for only a frac-
tion of the remuneration due).

Not only did this theft cut down on my employer's profits, it
also left me with practically no income after two weeks of work.
I reported the nephew's actions to my boss whose response was
only an exasperated shrug of the shoulders. When it became obvious after several more days of work that my employer had no
control over the nephew, I told him that I needed to find another
job. His response startled me. He yelled at me! He backed me into
a corner and tried to intimidate me into keeping the job without
any pay adjustments until he could find a replacement.

I was only sixteen, this was my first job ever, and my employer
tried to take advantage of my youth and inexperience to protect
his own interests. Thankfully, my father had told me he would
back me if I ran into any trouble. With my father's promise of support in mind, I was resolute not only in leaving the job but in
insisting that my employer pay the earnings he had promised but
did not stop his nephew from stealing. It all worked out, but rage
still fills me when I remember the unfairness of my boss.

My own heart's response to so distant an injustice makes it
abundantly clear that it is a great challenge to respond in a Christ-

like way to an employer's abuse. As a teenager, I had no family to protect, no career to promote, no years of investment in a company or its pension fund. I would have suffered very little, regardless of how the circumstances had unfolded. Yet if resentment can still reach me for such a slight matter so long ago, then I must confess that responding with Christ's character to an employer who damages family, career, and a future lies beyond the resolve my own heart can muster.

Sensing the limit of our abilities when we face Christian obligations to unjust employers, Peter does not say we must respond with hearts of love to these brutes, and for this we may be quick to utter a prayer of thanks. However, though he does not conclude his comments on dealing with masters with the allusion to Christian love that ended his earlier comments about our dealings with civil rulers, Peter concludes his instructions on all our relationships with these words: "Do not repay evil with evil or insult with insult, but with blessing, because to this you were called so that you may inherit a blessing" (1 Peter 3:9).

Not only do these imperatives forbid us to exclude our dealings with employers from Christian constraints; the instructions force us to consider how all our relationships must reflect Christ's own sacrifice on behalf of others. Such considerations touch the deepest corners of our hearts and ultimately drive us to determine how we live for Christ among those closest to us—those who have the potential to wound us most seriously.

Deeper Duty

Before making his final, sweeping statements that urge us to repay evil with blessing, Peter takes care to indicate how deep these obligations reach. Just as Christ submitted himself to suffering for our sakes (1 Peter 2:21–25), the apostle exhorts wives, "In the same way be submissive to your husbands" (3:1–6). Then he tells husbands to sacrifice the privileges of their authority and the advantages of their strength to the needs of their wives (v. 7).

We have heard these obligations described before but by placing them within the context of the Christian's wider obligations to others in society, Peter indicates how integrally related all our relationships are. We cannot divide our hearts in two, hoping that one part will serve in society and another will function separately in the home. Every place God calls us to serve helps form the character of our hearts and affects the way they will function in every other place. A heart that truly beats for others in society is the one most ready to live for others in the home. The heart that has learned sacrifice in the home is the one inclined to selflessness in the world.

By indicating that our obligations to God extend from government to the workplace to our families, Peter has effectively said that our Christian responsibilities apply to the entire spectrum of human relationships. Further, because those closest to us can hurt us the most deeply, Peter has indicated that these obligations remain no matter how difficult their application. Living for another does not cease to be an obligation because that one has ceased living for you.

A few years ago friends of ours followed standard legal advice given to young couples and had their wills prepared in case they should meet with untimely deaths. They accepted the responsibility of preparing for the proper care of their children but they still dreaded the morbid discussion with their attorney. The actual meeting with the attorney did little to remove their distaste for the matter. The important but difficult issues of what would happen if either, or both, were to die left the two feeling as though they were under a cloud. So in an effort to break the blue mood they were in, the wife tried to tease her husband a bit as they were leaving the lawyer's office. "Now, Sweetheart," she joked, "all we have to do to make one another rich is for one of us to die."

She was joking, but her husband did not laugh. He said, "Honey, don't ever talk that way. I can't even bear the thought of living without you. If we were ever separated, I would die." Though his tone was chastening, what he said was so warm an expression of love that the wife hugged her husband, wept, and promised never to talk like that again. Little did she suspect that within six months she would be weeping again because her husband had left her and his two children to live with another woman.

Betrayal by those closest to us cuts deep into our hearts and makes almost overwhelming the challenge to respond with attitudes and actions that reflect Christ's love. What would it mean for this wife and mother to repay evil with blessing as Peter instructs? Without knowing all that she must consider, I confess that I cannot answer. But this I do know: Her actions and attitudes toward her husband must demonstrate the reality of Christ in her. By these words I do not contend that a wife so abused may not seek the termination of her marriage in accordance with biblical guidelines,[2] but even this course may not be pursued without consideration of Christ's concerns and reflection of his character. Personal pain does not negate the Lord's call to repay evil and insult with blessing. Living for another necessitates sacrifice, and sometimes such sacrifices hurt a lot.

Duties to God

The reasons Christians sacrifice for others in home and society ultimately reside in the God we serve, not in the character of the people with whom we deal. With each obligation to serve people, the apostle lists a corresponding divine motive. In dealing with governing authorities Peter says that we must submit "for the Lord's sake" (1 Peter 2:13), resist foolishness by doing "God's will" (v. 15), live with integrity "as servants of God" (v. 16), and "fear God" while loving and honoring others (v. 17).

When these obligations to authorities are broadened and intensified in the context of our daily work, the apostle says that Christians must submit to masters by remaining "conscious of God" (v. 19), endure injustice since "this is commendable before God" (v. 20), and suffer with Christ-like love "because Christ suffered for you, leaving you an example, that you should follow in his steps" (v. 21).

Finally, as Peter applies these same principles to our homes, he reminds us that our most intimate relationships are aided by "reverence" (3:2), conducted "in God's sight" (v. 4), influence

166

the effectiveness of our prayers (v. 7), and (along with other relationships) are governed by a divine "calling" to bless others (vv. 8–9).

Now not only has the apostle heightened, widened, and deepened our obligations to others, but, by making us responsible to God, Peter has denied us any earthly excuse for avoiding these duties. The effects are twofold: We are kept from dancing, and we are kept from settling.

Kept from Dancing

When I write that our accountability to God keeps us from dancing, I am not speaking of the tango or the two-step. I refer to "the ol' Christian side step," the assumption that because someone else is not living up to his or her obligations, we can dispense with ours. Under such assumptions Christians reason, *Of course, it is proper to submit to governing authorities, unless they happen to be like our governing authorities.* Similar reasoning in the workplace asserts, *Of course, we should submit to employers, unless they have dealt with me unfairly, embarrassed me, or not given me my due.* In the home this rationale becomes, *Of course, I should live sacrificially for my spouse, unless he (or she) has treated me unkindly or made me feel small.* Each of these statements sidesteps the standards of Scripture on the basis that others' faults have removed our obligations.

The apostle makes it clear that regardless of the failings of the persons for whom we are responsible, Christ's standards still apply. We serve others not because they are deserving, but because we are responsible to our God. He will not allow us to dance away from our Christian duties because we do not like another's politics, do not appreciate a management style, or have been deeply hurt by someone we granted access to our hearts. Our God does not abandon us when we fail. He did not turn away from us when our wrongdoing caused him to undergo the pain of a cross. If we are reflecting Christ's character out of love for him, then we will not abandon care for others because they have caused us pain.

Kept from Settling

A second effect of raising human obligations to heaven's standards is that we are kept from settling for the goodness our own hands can grasp. As Christians begin to realize what Scripture truly requires, they understand more each day that the selfish motives and actions invading our relationships grieve our Savior. The honor, respect, and love for others that we should possess always lie beyond us. As we face the extent of our limitations, the imposing nature of the standards presented in Scripture echoes in the refrain of an old song: "They are so high I can't get over them, so wide I can't get 'round them, and so deep I can't get under them."

The requirements of a holy God press from us the hope that by our own strength we could meet the requirements of heaven or claim its blessings. This is not a hopelessness Christians ultimately regret, for only when we have fully faced the inadequacies of our own spiritual resources do we long for the saving grace of God.

The gold medalist high jumper in the 1992 Olympics cleared seven feet, eight and a half inches—an incredible feat! Yet, as impressive as that jump was, it was also a dramatic statement of human limitations. Not only did the winner of the gold medal jump the winning height, so did the silver medalist and so did the bronze medalist. What separated the winners was not their ability to clear the winning height but the number of tries they took to do so. What united the jumpers was their mutual inability to jump any higher. Seven feet, eight and a half inches was a "glass ceiling" these greatest of human athletes could not shatter. That height was the limit of human ability on that day.

The feats of the 1992 Olympic high jumpers and those who have since cleared even greater heights at other competitions boggle our minds. Still, as much as this sport demonstrates what the human mind, body, and will can accomplish, it demonstrates as clearly the boundaries of human potential. Although record leaps will probably continue to inch upward, no one will ever high jump a mile.

And no one will ever reach the standards of heaven by his or her own efforts. Peter wants us to understand this. By outlining the divine obligations we have in all our relationships, he makes us aware of our limits, even if our goodness is incredible by human standards.

Peter does not define our boundaries to frustrate us. On the contrary, he hopes to fix in us the faith that our Savior alone can take us to the spiritual heights he requires. The biblical imperatives "to act justly and to love mercy and to walk humbly with your God" (Micah 6:8) flow less easily from our lips when we see the breadth of human relationships in which Peter says Christ's followers must live out these obligations. The life situations in which the apostle calls us to sacrifice ourselves stretch the limits of human resolve to the breaking point. Peter knows personally the value of this brokenness and has spared none of our sensibilities to help us reach it. Quickly and mercifully his reasons unfold as we further examine his words.

Obligations Fulfilled

Jesus has already met for us the standards we cannot meet. In describing Christ's sacrificial ministry, Peter carefully reflects the perfection of the Savior's service in each dimension of our human obligation. Jesus, King of all creation, *submitted to the rule and the cruelty of human authorities* when he "suffered for you" at the hands of Jewish and Roman officials (1 Peter 2:21). He *endured foolish accusation and profound injustice* when he neither retaliated nor threatened those who "hurled their insults at him" (v. 23). Though faced with this monstrous unfairness, he *maintained a testimony of integrity* before God and man: "He committed no sin and no deceit was found in his mouth" (v. 22). Jesus performed each of these obligations *motivated by love:* "He himself bore our sins in his body on the tree" (v. 24). Although he had done no wrong, Jesus fulfilled every righteous standard that we find ourselves incapable of keeping. Though we are undeserving of his care, he remains faithful to us for our sakes.

Not only has our Savior stayed faithful to us despite our failings, he also remained completely faithful to our God by performing these duties. Rather than counting on human reward or regard to result from his sacrificial service, Jesus "entrusted himself to him who judges justly" (v. 23). With his obedience, Jesus *honored God alone*. He obeyed without the motive of personal gain and yielded his life entirely to the purposes and discretion of his Lord.

Everything our heavenly Father requires of us Jesus did. He acted justly, loved mercy, and walked humbly with his God. How this obedience aids us became evident to me in watching how another father cared for his child. This father was a student in one of my seminary classes. Because his wife had a doctor's appointment, this young man brought his four-year-old daughter to class one day. Obviously the child needed some distractions to occupy her through the hour-long class, and her dad was smart enough to bring toys and munchies to keep her content. All went fine until the bell rang for the next period.

Rushing for his next class, the father—who was now juggling a stuffed teddy bear, miscellaneous puzzle pieces, and a security blanket, along with his usual papers and books—dropped a container of Cheerios. As the cereal hoops spread across the floor, the now thoroughly flustered dad absentmindedly handed his knapsack full of heavy theology books to his daughter. "Hold this for me, honey," he said.

In less than half a second the little girl had assessed the weight of her burden. Her smile turned to a grimace as she looked to her father and cried, "Oh, Daddy, I can't. Please, help me." Immediately he took the burden and put it on his own shoulders. What the father required of his child, he took on himself.

Through the work of Jesus Christ, our God does the same. Recognizing that the standards of his holiness would overwhelm us, the Lord allowed his own Son to meet our righteous obligations. In the person of Jesus, our God put the burden of our obedience on himself. Our God not only requires our holiness, he also provides it.

Penalty Accepted

To make his supply complete, the Lord had to make provision for our failures as well as fulfill our obligations. The fact that Jesus met the obligations we owe does not negate the consequences of our sins. A close examination of our relationships will indicate that we all stand before God guilty of failure to live as he requires—whether by willful transgression or personal weakness. A holy God cannot ignore these faults. Our inability to meet our human and divine obligations results in separation from God because his approval of (or union with) what is sinful, unloving, or unholy would mean that he could not retain his own holiness. From the dawn of human history, God has made physical death the consequence of this separation from the giver and sustainer of life (see Gen. 2:17; 3:19). Our mortality reflects the deeper realities of eternal separation from God, which the Bible identifies as spiritual death for all who do not find a new source of life (see Rom. 6:23; Eph. 2:1; Heb. 9:14).

God himself grieves because of this separation and has released his people from its pain by putting the death penalty for our sin on his own Son. The very obedience by which Jesus fulfilled our righteous obligations uniquely qualified him to assume this penalty. Since "he committed no sin," he was in no debt to God. His righteousness had no limit and thus was of infinite worth. As a result, Jesus' sacrifice perfectly balances the heavenly books and cancels the penalty for all who ask God to account Christ's righteousness on their behalf. By God's decree, Christ accepts this penalty and sets us free from the consequences of our own sin (1 Peter 2:24; Isa. 53:10).

Peter cites the ways Jesus paid our penalty when his own righteousness released him from any obligation to suffer for sin. The apostle calls Christians to selfless sacrifice on the basis of Christ's example. "You should follow in his steps," says Peter (1 Peter 2:21). The words reveal an often-overlooked aspect of Christ's suffering. We can only follow in the steps of one who walked this earth. Peter's call reminds us that the King of the universe came to be born in disreputable circumstances, to live in an impoverished condition, to endure humiliating bondage to human laws, and to suffer a despicable death. The seventeenth-century Reformers captured the essence of this misery, writing: "Christ's humiliation consisted in his being born, and that in a low condition, made under the law, undergoing the miseries of this life, the wrath of God, and the cursed death of the cross; in being buried, and continuing under the power of death for a time."[3] By his passive submission to the conditions of this life and the consequences of our sin, Jesus' sufferings became payment for the penalty our sin deserves.

Still greater glory flows from heaven, and more gratitude floods our hearts, when we recognize Christ did not only *passively* suffer on our behalf. By restraining his divine powers, obeying the will of his Father, and delivering himself to his persecutors, Jesus *actively* sacrificed himself for us. Peter reports of Jesus, "He himself bore our sins in his body on the tree" (v. 24). In obedience to the will of his heavenly Father, Jesus gave himself to pay the penalty for our sins. Peter cites the result: "By his wounds you have been healed" (v. 24). By offering his life, Jesus gave us life.

From human accounts of people willing to sacrifice their lives for the well-being of another, we can begin to gauge the degree of love in Christ's willing acceptance of the penalty for our sin. In the winter of 1996 the *St. Louis Post-Dispatch* reported that fire had engulfed the home of a young family. Though such fires are routine, the story made the front page because of what was found in the fire. Apparently the young mother, Carla Jacob, awoke to the blaze only to discover that the rapidly advancing fire had blocked every path of escape for her and her two-month-old child. The mother quickly ran a few inches of water into the bathtub. She then placed the child faceup in the water and with her own body, Carla covered the child.

Firefighters found the two in the tub. The baby was alive. The mother had given her life for her child.

While we shudder at the sacrificial bravery of such a mother, we understand how such love beats in a mother's heart. What is far more difficult to understand—and shows the great extent of our Savior's love—is that he willingly gave his life for us despite the fact that our wrongdoing set the flames. He thrust his own body into hellish suffering to take on himself all the hurt of our failures, weaknesses, and willful disobedience to God. Though we act as his enemies in our wrongs, our Lord treated us as dearly loved children through his sacrifice (Rom. 5:8–10).

This is the greatest truth of the Christian faith. We are saved from the consequences of our sin by the sacrifice of Jesus. We need not pretend that we have been good enough to merit the eternal blessing of a holy God. We do not have to hide our eyes from our own errors and hope God does not notice. In the death of his Son, our God reveals to us the seriousness of our wrong and by that same sacrifice, he tells us how special we are to him.

By his perfect righteousness, Jesus became the perfect payment for the penalty our worst sins deserve. As we approach God, *not* on the basis of our wholly inadequate satisfaction of his requirements but on the basis of Christ's perfect fulfillment of our obligations, God accepts us as readily and completely as he does his own Son. We stand before him freed from all guilt because Jesus paid the debt we were unable to pay.

New Position

By virtue of Christ's work on our behalf, we assume a new spiritual position. The apostle Peter describes both negatively and positively our new existence as persons purchased eternally for God by the suffering of Jesus. First, Peter says what we are *not*. We are no longer "sheep going astray" (1 Peter 2:25). The allusion calls to mind images of rebellion, negligence, danger, destitution, and lostness. Each of these images is an aspect of the condition of sheep who wander from their shepherd and of people who depart from the care of the Savior. What unifies all of these aspects is that each is a dimension of the hurt a lamb inflicts on itself when it demands its own way.

In contrast to this hurt condition, Peter says that we who are drawn by the love of Jesus have returned "to the Shepherd and Overseer of [our] souls" (v. 25). When lost sheep return to the fold, their shepherd pours care and nurture on them. By describing our position as returning to the Shepherd of souls, the apostle encourages us to rejoice in the compassion of our Savior. Though our waywardness has brought us shame and pain, in Jesus' arms our hearts find solace and restoration.

Peter uses the shepherd image first so that we will understand what it means for us to return to the Overseer of our souls. Without the shepherd reference, the concept of an overseer could conjure thoughts of cruel or harsh domination. The apostle short-circuits such conclusions by introducing the shepherd imagery to confirm the Lord's love. This love is simply not static. A shepherd who recovers lost sheep does not want them endangered again. He takes steps to ensure their safety.

Our God's safekeeping involves standards and directions for our lives that protect our souls from the consequences of further sin. We have seen some of these standards of conduct in this passage. While attempts to follow these directives will not garner our salvation, they do direct us down paths God has designed to promote our good and his glory. Our wandering from this guidance does not remove the Savior's love from us, but it does take us from the way of blessing into brambles and briars of great hurt. By declaring Jesus the Overseer of our souls, the apostle reminds us of the loving direction Christ grants to our lives. Far from seeking to intimidate us with this reminder, the apostle informs us that the same God who beckons us with his care also protects us with his authority. When we honor Jesus as our Savior and the Lord of our lives, he rescues us from the guilt of our past sin *and* shields us from the ravages of a future without him.

A young couple who discovered all the aspects of God's care recently wrote to inform me how it had affected their lives:

> God used the example of his own sacrificial love for us to teach my wife and me what he requires in marriage, not just to demand our obedience but to shelter us in his love. Particularly helpful to me were the words of Ephesians 5:25—"Husbands, love your wives, just as Christ loved the church and gave himself up for her."
>
> God used this very passage to speak to me about my marriage with Pamela. About eight years ago we were struggling terribly and I saw our marriage fading fast as neither of us had any happiness (or anything else!). However, I was struck by how I was instructed to love Pamela as Christ loved the church. It occurred to me how faithful He always was to the church even as the church has so often been unfaithful and unpleasing to Him. I felt the Lord urging me as if saying, "Trust me for your happiness, but love your wife now!" I then trusted God with my happiness (to either give or not give) by obeying these words, and then the Lord had mercy

on us and gave to our marriage more happiness than I ever thought possible in any marriage. Oh, what a Savior . . . Oh, what a message we have for this world and God's people!

When each lives for the other, we not only share with another the love God has for that person, we also discover more of the love God has for us. In the position of care God secures for us, he protects us further by giving instructions that keep us in the safety of his paths and directions. Thus by serving as our Savior (who gave himself for us) and as our Lord (who gives direction to us), Jesus protects Christians from the penalty of their past errors and directs them away from further errors.

The way that Jesus shields us from our wrong helps us determine what the Bible describes as Christ's work of atonement. Seminary students memorize the Hebrew word for atonement by noting that it sounds like the English word *cover*. The association makes perfect sense because the biblical word designates the way God used a system of sacrifices in the Old Testament to shield (or cover) his people from the consequences of their sin. In a fuller sense, we understand how Christ's final sacrifice supplies an even more complete atonement for us. Under the cover provided at the cost of his blood, we are shielded from the guilt of our sin and sheltered from its continuance. This cover enables us to live eternally in the warmth of the heavenly Father's love. Further, our experience and expression of that sacrificial love serve as invitations to others to share in the same. God designs the selfless love of a husband and a wife to radiate outward—touching family members, church associations, societal relationships, and, ultimately, eternal souls. The God who gave himself for us now lets us participate in his plan to reach others with the message that his care will cover them forever. No biblical truth is more precious or compelling.

Under the Cover

When I was offered a year's sabbatical to write, I took my family to a cabin in the woods where normal duties would not encroach. Our time was made more wonderful by the rediscovery of how precious our family's moments together could be.

For the previous seven years we had raised our children in a huge house on my seminary's campus. This drafty, older house was really too large for us, but we had rattled around in it for so long that we did not recognize the distance it was putting between us. For most of every day we could virtually exist separately with only occasional glimpses of one another at mealtimes or while comparing schedules before dashing off to a meeting or school event. Thus we were in for quite an adjustment when we moved to the *one-room* cabin.

Our three children slept in the loft, while the main room below served as living quarters, kitchen, and parents' bedroom. The arrangement forced three early-rising kids back into a pattern they had long since abandoned when they thought they had gotten too old for cuddling. The cold of the cabin combined with the discomforts of the loft apparently made the warmth of Mom and Dad's bed irresistible. Our children suddenly rediscovered the delights of snuggling beneath the covers with their parents.

I hope you, my reader, will not consider me disrespectful for suggesting it is with echoes of this love that your heavenly parent now summons you into his care. Whether you have never known the shield God provides from your guilt or have wandered by your own tendencies from the shelter he provides, he beckons you under the cover made by his Son's atonement. Here lies the warmth of the eternal Father and rest for your soul. By turning from confidence in your righteousness and trusting in his provision alone, you too may come under the cover of his love.

As Christ's love covers your life, others will sense the warmth that Jesus gives you and will want to seek its comforts. Wherever the selfless love of Christ is lived—whether in a marriage, family, church, or societal relationships—more of his children will seek his warmth and will desire the comfort and the care of being there. Where each lives for the other according to Christ's love, another and another and another will have the opportunity to know that love as well.

nine

Each for the Other Forever

A friend of mine works as an ethno-linguist—he studies cultures through the way they communicate. His scientific studies are very interesting but offer him little opportunity for wealth and stardom. He has had to learn to reconcile himself to these limitations.

When he was in graduate school, the lack of lucrative potential began to bother my friend so much that he would lie awake at night plotting how to turn his knowledge into profit. The apparent answer came at a school social.

Graduate students from throughout the university attended the party. This led to some good-natured sparring among those from different departments about the value of their respective career tracks. My friend fared poorly in the verbal competition because hardly anyone knew what an ethno-linguist was, and several doubted if this field of study really had any real "science" behind it. Responding to a friendly challenge to prove the validity of his studies, my friend claimed that he could pick out the law students attending the party just by listening to their conversation. He succeeded! At the end of the party he had all of the lawyers-in-training fingered simply by the way they talked.

His success at the party crystallized my friend's plan for profit. He reasoned that since he could identify the speech pattern of lawyers, he should be able also to figure out how really successful lawyers talk. Then for fat fees he would teach this "successful speech" to attorneys hungry for their own career advancement. My friend was sure fame and fortune were right around the corner. His own studies soon convinced him otherwise.

He discovered that young lawyers and law students *sound* like lawyers. The most successful lawyers sound like *normal* people. The attorneys who really succeed depend on actions not words.

What is true of law is also true of love: those whose love succeeds depend on actions not words. That is really the core of the apostle John's message about our relationships. He writes:

> This is how we know what love is: Jesus Christ laid down his life for us. And we ought to lay down our lives for our brothers. If anyone has material possessions and sees his brother in need but has no pity on him, how can the love of God be in him? Dear children, let us not love with words or tongue but with actions and in truth.
>
> 1 John 3:16–18

The Problems with Words

The wisdom of the apostle echoes in our observations of marriages all around us. Merely saying the right words does not secure love. Everyone starts out saying the right words. All join in the familiar chorus:

"I love you."
"This is forever."
"I'll never forsake you."

Still, we know that saying these right words does not necessarily knit two lives together. The problem is not that people are dishonest in what they say. Almost no one lies when they repeat their vows of affection before the preacher. No one plans to have a miserable life. Everyone says, "I love you," and at that moment means it.

The problem is that couples cannot depend on words alone to keep them together. Words are too slippery. My wife and I went shopping for a washing machine a couple of years ago and discovered how words slip in meaning. We found out that if the capacity of a washer is listed as "large," that means small. If washers are listed as "extra large"—that means medium. Only washers with the words "super large" are large. The situation gets worse if you go looking for a mattress. The label "firm" means soft. The words "extra firm" signify kinda mushy. "Super firm" only means you're gettin' there. You do not find firm till you buy what our salesman called the "Imperial Superba-Firm II."

Words can also have different meanings for different people in their marriage commitments. For some "forever" means for a real long time. For others "till death does us part" means until our affections die. For some the promise to stay united "in sickness and in health" means as long as you don't make me too miserable for too long and the problems we face are not your fault.

It's not just that different people use the same words to mean different things. Our own words can change in meaning as our relationships change. A woman once told me how the words of her marriage changed, reflecting a changing relationship. She said, "When I was twenty-one, I cried when my husband said good-bye to go on a business trip, because I was so miserable when he was gone. When I was twenty-four, I cried when I heard him say hello, because I was so miserable when he was home. Before we were both thirty, I stopped crying and he stopped saying hello or good-bye, because I no longer cared whether he was home or gone."

Words are never enough to seal a love that lasts. The problem is *not* simply that we have difficulty calibrating the "forever" in the love that we promise each other. Our real challenge is defining the nature of the love that lasts. Words cannot adequately express this kind of love, much less secure it. The best poetry cannot encompass eternal love; our favorite song cannot really capture it; the most wonderful words inspired by feelings that we can hardly stand to breathe into sentences still do not say all that a ceaseless love must be. Words alone simply cannot bear love's weight over time. What we say to each other, or even what we say to ourselves about our feelings for each other, cannot guarantee a love that will last.

The Need for Actions

What secures true love if words cannot? The apostle answers when he says not to love with lip service but "with actions and in truth" (1 John 3:18). There is no question about the type of actions John has in mind. He explains this in a previous verse where he offers his own definition of love: "This is how we know what love is: Jesus Christ laid down his life for us" (v. 16).

John defines love by sacrifice. The preeminent example he offers is that of Jesus who willingly gave up his glory and privileges to suffer on the cross for your good and mine. John goes on to say that "we ought to lay down our lives" for each other (v. 16) and he offers the concrete example of sharing our material possessions with those in need as embodying this type of love (v. 17).

No mystery lies in applying these truths to marriage. The love that secures this most intimate of relationships must also be sacrificial. Of course God does not expect us physically to die for each other every day. We are, however, to die to self each day. The satisfaction of our own needs and desires cannot be the primary reason we enter, nor continue in, marriage. Such motives will never allow true love to flourish and endure.

An irony of this book on Christian marriage is that during its writing, my job has required that I be away from home more than at any other time in my marriage. Thus while I have written about the need for each spouse to live for the other, the daily care of our home and children has fallen to Kathy with unprecedented weight. To her have fallen household chores, financial bookkeeping, children's discipline, carpooling, and innumerable social obligations that to describe as "wearying" would be a gross understatement.

Through all of this, Kathy has refused to complain and, instead, has been my support when I have come home exhausted and occasionally frustrated. She has had every right to resent the extra duties heaped on her and to trumpet the unfairness of my absences. Kathy could easily broker her sacrifices into greater concern for herself or less ministry for me. When friends have encouraged "pity parties" because of "the great sacrifice" that she is making, she has asserted her desire to support my ministry and the necessity of this current phase of my work. Kathy and I have both privately shed some tears of loneliness and weariness. We have both longed for more time together. Overall, however, my absences have strangely strengthened our marriage as her selflessness during them has heightened my respect, appreciation, and love for her.

In Christian marriage each individual's actions have an *other* focus. Manipulation, intimidation, and deceit for personal gain have no place here. Such actions will destroy true love even if they secure personal advantages for a time. The Bible simply puts before us the wonderful mystery of human happiness that in the giving of self lie life's greatest gains. The greatest love grows where self is served the least. This mystery takes concrete form in marriage when we patiently endure one another's fears and foolishness, refuse to use strengths to take advantage of another's weaknesses, enable each to fulfill responsibilities, cheer one another's dreams, comfort each other's sorrows, work to understand each other's needs, and forgive one another.

The Truths That Count

These last words about forgiveness are important for they remind us that all these instructions *sound* easy until we disappoint, frustrate, or sin against each other—then loving actions become enormous challenges. Not only do we have trouble forgiving, but the very fact that we find this divine imperative a struggle reveals the spiritual weakness in each heart. That is why the apostle John tells us to love "in truth" as well as in deed. That "truth" involves more than dealing with one another in integrity. Each of us must also face a vital truth about ourselves: We are far less capable of selfless love than we dare to confess.

To care for another more than we do for ourselves runs counter to our nature. Personal satisfaction, control, and advancement dominate our thoughts and pursuits. Even our care for one another cannot rid itself of the motives of recompense and recognition. If you do not believe this, then simply remember the rage that filled your heart the last time you went the extra mile for a spouse or a child and no one said thank you.

Our general expectation of some return on the love we invest in another reminds us that genuine affection and willing sacrifice may still have significant measures of self in them. In fact purely selfless love eludes us all. For who would contend that in their marriages they never do or desire anything that requires their being served by the actions or responses of a spouse? What the apostle has told us to *be* in our marriages is *beyond* us. Each of us fails the requirement never to manipulate, intimidate, or use another.

This truth is most evident when we consider *why* Christ died. John tells us about the sacrifice of Jesus, not merely to give us an example to mimic but to remind us of our guilt that he must cover. Yet in this reminder there is more than the exposure of truth about us; there is also the revelation of a God who is *for* us. In the sacrifice of his Son, our God reveals his selfless desire to bless his children. Our God gains nothing in the deal of providing his Son to take the penalty for our guilt. His love is more selfless than that of a mother nursing her baby. She gives of herself to the child, who can do nothing for her. Our God has given his own life for us, even though we are as helpless as infants to benefit him.

Full understanding of our Lord's selflessness ultimately engenders in us those attributes lacking in our own love that will make it last. First, as we humbly contemplate the forgiveness that God freely gives us, we discover how hypocritical it is to receive undeserved pardon and, then, not offer it (see Matt. 18:21–35). Then, in recognition of our own need for forgiveness, we discover the willingness to forgive that heals and seals our relationships. This is why love has a chance despite the inescapable truth of personal selfishness that we each must confess.

A wedding sealed by forgiveness took place recently near New York City. A young Asian-American woman had invited her father to her wedding despite his abandonment of her mother nearly thirty years earlier when the family had arrived in the United States. As part of the wedding tradition in their country of origin, the father was to be served a meal by the young woman's mother.

Though she was a Christian, the mother protested. When her husband had left her destitute with three small children many years before, she had labored unceasingly in menial jobs to support them. At the same time she was earning multiple degrees at prestigious universities. Ultimately she earned a doctorate in child psychology and established a clinic of national repute to treat troubled children. For her, the thought of serving the man who had treated her so despicably was repulsive and humanly impossible.

For the sake of their daughter both mother and father came to the wedding. Still, the mother made no commitment to serve the father as tradition required. She watched her husband enter the wedding room with an arrogant stride, as if he deserved to be there. She listened to him speak to relatives without shame or apology for the misery he had caused his own family. His every action and word increased the temperature of the thirty years of resentment in her.

Until the actual moment in the ceremony when the ritual meal was to occur, the mother would not agree to participate in the service. Then, though it surprised her as much as it did the others in attendance, the mother took the ceremonial bowl of rice, knelt before her husband, and served him. The rice she put on his plate was moistened by her tears. "They were not tears of pain," she later said, "but of inexpressible joy."

She explained, "When I let go of my anger enough to serve my husband, it was as though I understood for the first time how much Jesus loves me. I understood the pain he endured not to hold my eternal guilt against me, but to serve me by giving his own life for me. When I served my husband, I felt the love of my Savior flood into my heart and wash away thirty years of fury that had embittered me and enslaved my heart. In forgiveness I found freedom from the misery in my heart that I had not been able to erase with all of my achievements."

More was achieved by the forgiveness she displayed than the mother initially knew. When the daughter witnessed the self-lessness of her mother, she later said that for the first time she believed that the love of God was so real that it could have power in her own marriage. The daughter's unvoiced fear that her faults or her husband's would ultimately destroy their happiness, as it had her parents', evaporated in the knowledge that Christ's for-giveness could be shared. The forgiveness the mother demon-strated freed her own heart to love again, and sealed the love of her daughter's marriage.

As wonderful as it is to discover and share the truths of our Savior's forgiveness, this is not the end of our blessing. As we for-give others and our perception of the reality of our Savior's par-don deepens, our desire to honor him naturally increases. Then as we honor him with our lives, something else very special hap-pens. We discover to our delight that by loving the Lord who cre-ated marriage, our love for our spouses has the greatest opportu-nity to grow.

When our first son was small, he loved to walk through the church parking lot between his mother and me. We would each hold one of his hands, and then on cue he would lift his feet. He would giggle while his legs dangled in the air between us. But he would whoop for pure joy when we would swing him back and forth until his feet actually went above our heads. The higher we swung him, the greater was his delight.

Something else also happened with each swing of our child. Not only did we lift our son higher, but we were inevitably drawn closer together by the physical forces engaged in doing so. When two lives in a marriage lift the Son of God in honor, similar dynam-ics occur—the higher we lift him, the closer together we grow. By honoring him, our hearts are changed, our priorities come more in line with his purposes, our selfishness withers, and our for-giveness grows. We begin to tolerate each other's weaknesses more because we recognize our need for Christ's sufficiency in our own weaknesses. Our mutual understanding of each other deepens because we are each becoming more like Christ.

A Third Party

The commitments that we make in marriage are not merely agreements between two people. Christ, in actively renewing and deepening the love that we share, is also a party to our relationship. This truth further secures Christian marriages.

When we vow to love and honor each other, we also make these promises *before* and *to* our God. This means that even when words and feelings between the two people fail to keep the marriage that God desires, we should not consider the marriage finished. Our promises to remain perpetually committed to each other are ultimately made to God.

If we have given our lives to the purpose of reflecting God's character and commitments, then in our marriage vows we promise God that we will live for the other person. God does not make his love conditional on the way we feel about him, on how we treat him, or on whether we have failed him. Thus neither the cooling of our affections for another, nor the heat of stress with that person excuses us from our marriage commitments. We live for another because we have committed ourselves to living for the God who requires it. We love another because we promised the God we love that we would.

Because the actions that keep a Christian couple united are linked to their eternal commitments to God, their marriage becomes a haven for the constant renewal of love rather than a trap to escape when an initial ardor dies. The man and woman need not be constantly questioning if either will say or do something that destroys their relationship; rather they proceed to live with freedom and boldness in the knowledge that their mutual commitment to God has secured their home more surely than their affections ever could. Yet, curiously, it is this very security that gives their affections the greatest potential to deepen. Committing to love another person beyond his or her weaknesses, to work on a relationship despite difficulties and differences, and to live for the other because that's what God requires, gives love the richest soil possible in which to flourish.

Only weeks after Kathy and I were married, we had one of the most difficult arguments of our lives. Interestingly, I cannot now even remember what the subject was. All I can remember were the hours of discussion, the mounds of tear-drying tissues heaped on the bed, the lateness of the evening, and Kathy's final question: "If we have this kind of difference between us, is our marriage over?"

I then did one of the stupidest things that I have ever done in my life. I laughed—not just a chuckle—a deep, long, bellyaching, sidesplitting roar. I am sure that my reaction was, in part, an involuntary release of the tension built up in me, but it was also a response to how hilarious I considered Kathy's question. The thought had never entered my mind that our differences were a threat to our marriage. I loved Kathy more than I could well express. I was looking forward to spending a lifetime with her. I had promised God that I would love her regardless of difficulty. The suggestion that an argument might undo us struck me as so off the wall and bizarre that I could not help but laugh.

I am not suggesting that my laughing was the right thing to do, but God graciously used it that night to reassure Kathy of the security of our relationship. Seeing that the idea of some disagreement separating us was so foreign to me that I could not keep from laughing at it gave her a sense of how secure she was in our relationship. Her knowledge of that security made her more willing to bring up other things in the future that we needed to discuss. These were not always pleasant discussions but they enabled us to deal with matters that ultimately have made our marriage far stronger and sweeter.

God used Kathy's and my commitment to him to make our marriage so secure that we could work on our weaknesses, growing past them to increase the quality of our love for each other. We still have much growing that we need to do. But we do not fear growing because God has taught us that by committing our lives to honoring him, we invite his care into our marriage to help deepen our love for him and each other. His care brings us closer with each passing year, not only through the unusual (like my laughter) but by placing us in situations that enable us to understand each other better. He lets us see how our lives can touch others, and so we learn to appreciate each other's gifts. He unites our hearts to pray for our children's battles and blessings and he gives us enough trials to keep us tender with enough joys to keep us hugging. In all of this the bond of love between us is strengthened.

We cannot say that we know how it has happened at every step, but Kathy and I marvel that in each phase of our marriage we grow closer and consider our relationship a greater blessing. We know too much about our own weaknesses to credit ourselves for this grace. We simply praise God that when we were weak, he was strong. He used our commitments to him to bind us closer to each other. For this reason we humbly rejoice that we will never be like those couples who look back on their wedding days or their first years together as the best time of their marriages. As we have continued to commit our marriage to God, our love gets better and better. Our prayer and the purpose of this book is to help others partake of similar blessings.

Consider that no matter how happy your marriage is now, this may only be the beginning of the joy that you can know as you entrust your lives to the Lord. He will use your shared love for him to increase your love for each other. And in marriages where love for God is not shared, God can still use your love for your spouse to deepen your appreciation of God's unconditional care for you, to teach your spouse the nature of God's care through you, and even to stimulate in your spouse renewed love for God and you (see 1 Peter 3:1–2).

Such sacrificial love is not secured by words that we mouth nor even by actions that we initiate under some romantic impulse to make another (or ourselves) feel good. The love that is truly secure stems from hearts united with God. Because words can ring hollow and actions can spring from motives hidden even to the one who acts, only our hearts' commitments to Christ will turn our words and actions into the marriage we most desire. Our spiritual commitments—what is deepest in our hearts rather than the outward expressions of words or deeds—ultimately will secure what is dearest in our lives.

We should not be surprised that what is inside is most important. Our experience regularly tells us to beware of external appearances when assessing true integrity. When the tragedy of the *Challenger* space shuttle shook our nation in 1986, investigators went to amazing lengths to discern the cause. Ultimately they found that in the unusually cold temperatures of that day, gaskets—known as O-rings—around the engines had failed. The failure caused a fuel leak that ignited and led to the shuttle's explosion.

Initially this analysis surprised some at NASA because inspectors had externally examined the O-rings just prior to the flight. Everything looked fine on the outside. What the disaster investigation revealed was that the external inspection was not meaningful. The tragedy was due to failures on the inside of those rings where no one could see.

On our wedding days, most of us assume the wearing of other "O-rings." The words that we say and the actions that we take to put the golden bands in place make everything appear fine on the outside. We must remember that what is inside counts more. The commitment of our hearts to the grace of God ultimately makes our words and actions truly and eternally loving. Living for the one who loved us when we were yet his enemies teaches us what it means for each to live for the other in marriage when no other earthly cause may justify our continuing union. The Lord who died for us teaches us that when we give of ourselves for another—dying to ourselves in the process—we discover what it really means to live, and enjoy most fully what it really means to love. Our Lord makes our lives as sweet as heaven desires by drawing our hearts together in love for him.

Discussion Questions

Introduction: Who's in Charge?

1. What motivations other than sacrifice can govern the relationships of men and women?
2. How does the grace of God become a reality in our homes through sacrifice?
3. Why does knowledge of Bible facts alone not adequately prepare us for the home life God intends?
4. What will adequately prepare us for the home life God intends?
5. What are challenges in our society to the Bible's instruction for the family?
6. Why is self-sacrifice the cornerstone of the Bible's architecture for the Christian home?
7. Does living for another require an abandonment of one's integrity or authority?

Chapter 1: A Man's Responsibility

1. How does Paul compare the relationship of a husband and wife to that of Christ and the church?
2. How does the biblical concept of "headship" contradict philosophies of self-serving male passivity or dominance?
3. In what sense does biblical headship involve authority?

4. In what sense does biblical headship involve service?
5. What is a servant/leader? Who best models this role in Scripture? How?
6. In what ways does the head of a home dispense grace into the home?

Chapter 2: God's Reasons for Servant Leadership

1. How is the servant/leader role of a husband related to the redemptive purposes of marriage?
2. In what sense is improper biblical headship spiritual robbery?
3. Why is the devaluing of one's spouse always spiritually self-destructive? To whom is it spiritually destructive? Why?
4. In what sense does a wife complete her husband? How does this affect a man's expression of biblical headship?
5. What are ways that a husband can honor his wife? Why is it important to do so? How does a husband's honoring of his wife affect him?
6. In what ways does biblical headship honor God?

Chapter 3: God's Resources for Servant Leadership

1. How is selflessness a resource for husbands to express headship in the home?
2. How can husbands foster growth in their wives? Why should husbands do this?
3. How does a husband's character affect the spiritual health of his wife?
4. Does the Bible mandate a specific manner or personality for the proper expression of headship?
5. In what way does one's relationship with Christ affect one's ability to act as the biblical head of a home? How is humility related to headship?
6. What kinds of insecurities may cause a man to want his wife dependent on him?

7. When and why is it good for a husband to lose an argument (or discussion)?
8. How does the leadership and sacrifice of Christ instruct husbands in their headship role?

Chapter 4: A Woman's Responsibility

1. What analogy and example does Paul use to express how wives should submit to their husbands?
2. To what extent does the apostle say wives should submit to husbands?
3. Is the instruction given in this passage to husbands and wives culturally limited? What is the basis for your conclusion?
4. In what sense does biblical submission require one to complete another?
5. In what sense does biblical submission require one to glorify another?
6. Does submission require the suppression of one's gifts, talents, and abilities? If not, why not?
7. Are there any limits to how one's gifts, talents, and abilities should be expressed? If so, what are these limits and how are they determined?

Chapter 5: A Woman's Dignity

1. How does biblical submission grant a wife dignity?
2. Does biblical submission lessen the value or worth of anyone in God's estimation? If not, why not?
3. In what ways does a focus on promoting ourselves rob us of dignity?
4. Why are almost any career or family choices a woman makes in today's world attackable?
5. How should the church affirm the dignity and gifts of Christian women?

6. How should a Christian husband demonstrate respect for a wife who lives in accord with Scripture?

Chapter 6: A Woman's Desire

1. In what ways are wives tempted to neglect or break Scripture's command to respect their husbands?
2. In what ways should Christian wives respect their husbands? Why?
3. How can a woman respect a husband who is not worthy of such regard?
4. How can a woman respect a man who does not respect her? Should she respect such a man? In what ways?
5. What does the Bible mean when it tells Christian wives to "reverence" their husbands? Why do you think the apostle uses this language?
6. What influence does a godly wife exert on her family, church, and community? How important is this influence?

Chapter 7: Each for the Other as Parents

1. In what ways does our perception of God as our Father shape the parents we are able to be?
2. In what ways does our security (or insecurity) in Christ affect our parenting?
3. How does the relationship of a husband and wife bring the reality of Christ's love into a home? How important is this influence on a child?
4. To whom does Scripture give the responsibility for child rearing? How should this responsibility affect parents' priorities regarding their work, energy, time, and attention?
5. Which parent is ultimately accountable for a child's nurture in a two-parent household? Does this mean that one parent is not accountable for a child's nurture? Explain.

6. What does the apostle mean when he instructs parents, "Do not exasperate your children"? What are ways parents exasperate their children?

7. How is firm but kindly discipline prescribed in Scripture? How is it manifested in parenting? How is it mangled in parenting?

Chapter 8: Each for the Other in Society

1. What obligations do Christians have to governing authorities, to employers, and to spouses?

2. In what ways do (or should) Christian obligations *within* the home affect the relationships we have outside the home?

3. In what ways do (or should) Christian obligations *outside* the home affect relationships inside the home?

4. How are our obligations to persons in and out of the home further heightened by our obligations to God?

5. What does the height, width, and depth of our spiritual obligations ultimately reveal about the limits of our goodness?

6. How does God keep us from despairing about the limits of our own spiritual abilities?

7. In what ways did Jesus fulfill our spiritual obligations?

8. How did Jesus accept the penalty for our spiritual failures? What were the passive and active dimensions of this acceptance?

9. In what ways should we honor Jesus as a result of his atonement for our sin?

10. Have you experienced what it means to be "covered" by the care that Christ provides? If not, do you understand how you can know his care when you acknowledge him as your Savior and live for him in gratitude for the way he gave himself for you?

Chapter 9: Each for the Other Forever

1. Why can words not secure a marriage, even if we mean them?
2. What kinds of actions secure love?
3. How does Christ's forgiveness of us affect our actions toward our spouses?
4. Who is the third party in every marriage vow, and how does this person affect our marriage commitments?
5. Why does a person's commitment to Christ affect his or her words and actions in marriage?
6. Why should one spouse live out his or her commitments to Christ if the other spouse does not?
7. How can married love keep getting better and better?

Notes

Introduction: *Who's in Charge?*

1. Figures published by the Heritage Foundation in *Christianity Today* (September 13, 1993): 32. Figures vary in the *Statistical Abstract of the United States*, edition 116, published by the U.S. Bureau of Census, 1996 (pp. 79 and 104), but still confirm that the foundations of the American family have been significantly eroded by the cultural tides of the last three decades. Some of the government statistics were actually worse than those reported by the Heritage Foundation, e.g., percentage of births to unwed mothers in 1994—the latest available—was 31 percent.

Chapter 1: *A Man's Responsibility*

1. The man is also described as the head of the woman in 1 Cor. 11:3–10. Other key passages on this subject include Gen. 2:18–25; 3:16; 1 Cor. 14:33–35; Col. 3:18; 1 Tim. 2:8–15; Titus 2:3–5; 1 Peter 3:1–6.

2. James B. Hurley, *Man and Woman in Biblical Perspective* (Grand Rapids: Zondervan, 1981), 167–81, 254–71.

3. These issues are well explored and explained in Hurley, *Man and Woman in Biblical Perspective*, 181–84; S. M. Baugh, "A Foreign World: Ephesus in the First Century," in *Women in the Church: A Fresh Analysis of 1 Timothy 2:9–15*, ed. Andreas J. Kostenberger, Thomas H. Schreiner, and H. Scott Baldwin (Grand Rapids: Baker, 1995), 47–48; Thomas H. Schreiner, "An Interpretation of 1 Timothy 2:9–15: A Dialogue with Scholarship," in *Women in the Church*, 117–21; John Piper and Wayne Grudem, "An Overview of Central Concerns," in *Recovering Biblical Manhood and Womanhood*, ed. John Piper and Wayne Grudem (Wheaton: Crossway, 1991), 65–67, 74–75; Edmund P. Clowney, *The Church*, in *Contours of Christian Theology*, gen. ed. Gerald Bray (Downers Grove, Ill.: InterVarsity Press, 1995), 215–35.

4. William J. Larkin Jr., *Culture and Biblical Hermeneutics* (Grand Rapids: Baker, 1988), 109.

5. A noteworthy early article thrusting this idea into popular evangelical discussion is Berkeley and Alvera Mickelsen, "The 'Head' of the Epistles," *Christianity Today* 25, no. 4 (February 20, 1981): 21ff. Similar discussions appear in the Mickelsens' later work, "What Does *Kephale* Mean in the New Testament?" in *Women, Authority and the Bible*, ed. Alvera

Mickelsen (Downers Grove, Ill.: InterVarsity Press, 1986), 97–110. Other related articles also appear in this source, pages 111–32, 134–54. See also Catherine Clark Kroeger, "The Classical Concept of *Head* as 'Source,'" appendix 3 in Gretchen Gaebelein Hull, *Equal to Serve* (Old Tappan, N.J.: Revell, 1987), 267–83.

6. Michael Ovey, "Equality but Not Symmetry: Women, Men and the Nature of God," *The Cambridge Papers* 1, no. 2 (June 1992): 2–3.

7. Wayne Grudem, "Does *Kephale* ('Head') Mean 'Source' or 'Authority Over' in Greek Literature? A Survey of 2,336 Examples," in *The Role Relationship of Men and Women,* ed. George Knight III (Chicago: Moody, 1985), 50. See also Grudem's later discussion in Piper and Grudem, *Recovering Biblical Manhood and Womanhood,* 63–64, 425–68; and Susan T. Foh, *Women and the Word of God: A Response to Biblical Feminism* (Phillipsburg, N.J.: Presbyterian and Reformed, 1979), 101–2.

8. F. F. Bruce, *The Epistle to the Colossians, to Philemon, and to the Ephesians* (Grand Rapids: Eerdmans, 1984), 384. Further reasons for the "authority" translation are discussed by Thomas H. Schreiner, Harold O. J. Brown, and Daniel Doriani in *Women in the Church,* ed. Kostenberger, Schreiner, and Baldwin, 135–46, 200–206, 259–67.

9. Though more able language scholars than I have studied this question, it appears to me that the term *head* may in certain verses *include* the idea of source (see Hurley, *Man and Woman in Biblical Perspective,* 144–47, 164–68). However, when this is the case, "source" is not the exclusive meaning of the term but rather is a corollary meaning contributing rationale to why the head has authority (see 1 Cor. 11:8–10; Eph. 4:14–16; Col. 1:18; 2:19). Grudem has a similar conclusion in Piper and Grudem, *Recovering Biblical Manhood and Womanhood,* 468. See also S. Bedale, "The Meaning of Kephale in the Pauline Epistles," *Journal of Theological Studies* 5 (1954): 211–15 as cited in Hurley, *Man and Woman in Biblical Perspective,* 164; and the note on Ephesians 5:23 in the *New Geneva Study Bible,* gen. ed., R. C. Sproul (Nashville: Thomas Nelson, 1995), 1869.

10. Hurley, *Man and Woman in Biblical Perspective,* 168.

11. R. Kent Hughes, *Ephesians: The Mystery of the Body of Christ* (Wheaton: Crossway, 1990), 181–82.

12. Hurley, *Man and Woman in Biblical Perspective,* 240–42.

13. The string of participles composing this long Greek sentence, though translated as imperatives, are actually descriptions of the necessary characteristics of those "filled with the Spirit."

14. Significantly different interpretations have been given to the loving phrase "submit to one another." Some have taken the phrase to mean that among Christians no one should have any authority over anyone. This interpretation seems unlikely since wives are immediately told to submit to their husbands, children are told to obey parents, and slaves (better interpreted as "servants"; see note 3 in chapter 5) are told to obey earthly masters. In addition, Paul here and elsewhere establishes offices of authority in the church (see Eph. 4:11; 1 Tim. 5:17).

Other respected interpreters examine the use of these words elsewhere and conclude the phrase applies only to those who are in submissive roles (see Hurley, *Man and Woman in Biblical Perspective,* 140–44; Piper and Grudem, *Recovering Biblical Manhood and Womanhood,* 493–94 [footnote 6]). This may seem to indicate that the only ones who have submission obligations are those in subservient positions. While I understand the concern these conscientious authors have not to blur biblical husband/wife distinctions by allowing that husbands are to "submit" to their wives, questions remain about their interpretation. Reasons for such questions include: (1) the long Greek sentence (Eph. 5:18–21) that includes this requirement of submission also includes three other requirements that apply to *all* in the church rather than one group of persons; (2) each of these requirements is a consequence of individuals being "filled with the Spirit"—a quality *all* believers are to desire; (3) and the commands for *all* persons that follow (including husbands, parents, and masters) make it clear that putting self-interest beneath the interests of others is required of every believer (see George W. Knight III, "Husbands and Wives as Analogues of Christ and the Church: Ephesians 5:21–33 and Colossians 3:18–19," in Piper and Grudem, eds., *Recovering Biblical Manhood and Womanhood*, 167–68). Arguing that the Greek word for submission "is never 'mutual' in its force; it is *always one-directional* in its reference to submission to authority" (Piper and Grudem, 493) does not negate the possibility that submission requirements apply to all believers since each is acting "out of reverence for Christ" and thus all are ultimately submitting to the one divine authority.

My understanding is that Paul intended for the general phrase "submitting to one another out of reverence for Christ" to apply to all in the church as each lives sacrificially in every position or relationship God provides. However, with precisely inspired balance and to avoid confusion about roles and responsibilities, the apostle never uses the "submit" term when directly instructing husbands, parents, and masters about their relationships with those under their authority. The issues are complex, however, and I freely concede an unwillingness to claim certainty on the particular point of whether the specific "submit" term applies to those in authority. Still, this discussion about whether the specific term applies to all persons in every relationship, should not make anyone uncertain about Paul's clear statement at the outset of this passage that all believers should "live a life of love, just as Christ loved us and gave himself up for us" (Eph. 5:2). This foundation principle makes it clear that *all* persons are to sacrifice their own interests to the purposes of God as they are being fulfilled in others.

The general requirement of personal selflessness is reemphasized when the apostle later tells those in authority to give of themselves for the good of those under their care. Hence, husbands are told to love their wives "just as Christ loved the church and gave himself up for her" (5:25; and note also that this is precisely how women are told to "submit" in 1 Peter 3:1; cf. 3:7); fathers are told, "do not exasperate your children" (Eph. 6:4); and masters are commanded "in the same way" not to threaten their servants since "he who is both their Master and yours is in heaven, and there is no favoritism with him" (v. 9). Paul does not obliterate all authority but rather requires all persons of every distinction to surrender their own advantages and benefits to the good of the ones for whom they are responsible. The closest analogy to this kind of submission is the very one that Paul is citing; i.e., in love Christ served the church by sacrificing himself in her behalf, but in terms of authority he did not serve the church in the same way that she submits to him. He maintained his authority even as he humbled himself to offer his life for the church's good (Phil. 2:5–11). For expert discussion of this careful balance see Foh, *Women and the Word of God*, 134.

15. Note also that since the pivotal verses in the Ephesians passage (which require loving sacrifice of all persons in all positions) hold the controlling thought for the concepts that follow, it is appropriate that "servant" have the priority position in the servant/leader terminology (Eph. 5:1–2, 18–21).

16. Hughes, *Ephesians*, 184.

Chapter 2: *God's Reasons for Servant Leadership*

1. Geoffrey C. Ward with Ric Burns and Ken Burns, *The Civil War: An Illustrated History* (New York: Alfred A. Knopf, 1990), 82–83.

2. Writes Charles E. Mylander, "Beware of emotional delight outside of marriage that is not taking place within it. An emotional affair precedes a physical one. The first step toward adultery is discovering a special pleasure with someone of the opposite sex other than one's spouse. During this 'conversation stage' everything seems innocent and fun—until the friendship begins to seem more fulfilling than your marriage." See Charles E. Mylander, "Running the Yellow Lights," *Marriage Partnership* 4, no. 6 (November–December 1987): 36–38.

3. Though sometimes ridiculed as "the gift nobody wants," the Bible identifies celibacy (i.e., living singly because of the circumstances or calling God has arranged for one's life) as an honored relationship with God. Those God calls to singleness as evidenced by their desires or their circumstances are the only ones who are designed (i.e., gifted) by God to be complete without being in union with a spouse. Such persons are, in a special sense, married to God. They find their wholeness in him without the need of another's help or support in the marital union (see Gen. 2:18; 1 Cor. 11:11). As a result, those gifted for singleness are specially equipped to serve God without the encumbering responsibilities the married must consider (see Matt. 19:10–12; 1 Cor. 7:4–7, 25–38). The Bible does not indicate that any calling is without its challenges, but the fact that celibacy is a gift of God grants the status honor and dignity despite the attitudes of a society or the struggles of those who are single.

Elisabeth Elliot writes, "The gift of virginity, given to everyone to offer back to God for His use, is a priceless and irreplaceable gift. It can be offered in the pure sacrifice of marriage, or it can be offered in the sacrifice of a life's celibacy. Does this sound just too high and holy? But think a moment—because the virgin has never known a man, she is free to concern herself wholly with God's affairs, as Paul said in 1 Corinthians 7, 'and her aim in life is to make herself holy, in body and spirit.' She keeps her heart as the Bride of Christ in a very special sense, and offers to the Heavenly Bridegroom alone all that she is and has. When she gives herself willingly to Him in love she has no need to justify herself to the world or to Christians who plague her with questions and suggestions. In a way not open to the married woman her daily 'living sacrifice' is a powerful and humble witness, radiating love. I believe she may enter into the 'mystery' more deeply than the rest of us." See "Virginity," *Elisabeth Elliot Newsletter* (Ann Arbor, Mich.: Servant Publications [March–April 1990]): 2–3.

4. Tertullian, as quoted in David and Vera Mace, *What's Happening to Clergy Marriages?* (Nashville: Abingdon, 1980), 97.

Chapter 3: *God's Resources for Servant Leadership*

1. Karen Howe, "Husbands, Forget the Heroics!" *Eternity* 25, no. 12 (December 1974): 11.

2. Robertson McQuilkin, "Living by Vows," *Christianity Today* 39, no. 14 (October 8, 1990): 38–40.

3. Paul Tournier, *To Understand Each Other* (Richmond: John Knox, 1967), 22–26, 38–42.

4. Howe, "Husbands, Forget the Heroics!" 12.

5. The first response in the historic *Westminster Shorter Catechism* is "Man's chief end is to glorify God and enjoy him forever." See Matthew 22:37.

6. "He has showed you, O man, what is good. And what does the LORD require of you? To act justly and to love mercy and to walk humbly with your God" (Micah 6:8). See earlier definitions of biblical headship, pp. 31–37.

7. Robertson McQuilkin, "Muriel's Blessing," *Christianity Today* 40, no. 2 (February 5, 1996): 34.

8. McQuilkin, "Living by Vows," 40.

Chapter 4: *A Woman's Responsibility*

1. Hal Farnsworth, now a pastor in Athens, Georgia.

2. Cf. Gen. 2:18–25; 3:16; 1 Cor. 11:3ff.; 14:33–36; Eph. 5:22–33; Col. 3:18; 1 Tim. 2:8–15; Titus 2:3–5; 1 Peter 3:1–6.

3. Cf. 1 Peter 2:17; 3:7. The New Testament word for *respect* in these passages has a range of meaning determined by context as does our modern equivalent (for example, children who respect their father and respect the president are not expected to hum "Hail to the Chief" each time Dad enters a room). Nevertheless, the Bible makes it clear that husbands must treat their wives with the consideration due those for whom Christ gave his blood.

4. The Greek word for submission is a combination of *tasso,* meaning, "to arrange," "to put in order," or "to command," and *hupo,* meaning "under." Still, we must take care to interpret all words in the Bible not merely in accord with their background meanings but in the light of their context and biblical use. Standard Greek references will interpret *hupotasso* in the forms that occur in these passages as meaning "to be subject, subordinate, or submissive." See Hurley, *Man and Woman in Biblical Perspective,* 142–46.

5. Piper and Grudem, "An Overview of Central Concerns," 61; Knight, "Husbands and Wives," 166; Schreiner, "An Interpretation of 1 Timothy 2:9–15," 125. Note this last definition is based on the parallel phrasing in 1 Timothy 2:11–12.

6. Marion Stroud, *I Love God and My Husband* (Wheaton: Victor, 1973), 53.

7. Virtually all commentators quickly add that submission is not an unqualified mandate to obey a spouse if such submission would require transgression of God's standards. See Foh, *Women and the Word of God,* 184. Susan Hunt writes, "Women are not to submit to sin. Sometimes it is very clear when that line has been crossed. Sometimes the line, or the vision of the line, is blurred. When the authority of the husband cannot be trusted, I encourage women to seek the advice, authority, and protection of the elders of her church" (Susan Hunt, *The True Woman* [Wheaton: Crossway, 1997], 206).

8. See earlier discussion in chapter 2 on the "gift of celibacy" and Foh, *Women and the Word of God,* 128–29.

9. See, for example, Psalms 10:14; 28:7 (in Hebrew); 54:3–4; 72:12; 86:17. Susan Hunt in *The True Woman* comments on the impact of such references for wives: "This explanation of how God is our ezer [Helper] gives us insight into the helper role. The ways that God is our Helper can be summarized into two categories: community and compassion. God enters into a loving, protecting relationship with his people (community). He comes to our aid, comforts us and is merciful toward us (compassion). . . . This touches our feminine souls because our entering into nurturing relationships, and extending compassion to those in need, is part of our helper design. Our design equips us to infuse community and compassion into our relationships. Women will do this in various ways. We are not clones. Our strengths, temperaments, experiences, opportunities, life-stage, and interests will be factors in how we fulfill this design" (p. 206). For an explanation of how the "helper" term does not imply inferiority, see Foh, *Women and the Word of God,* 60.

10. Elisabeth Elliot, "The Essence of Femininity: A Personal Perspective," in *Recovering Biblical Manhood and Womanhood,* 397.

11. This understanding fits with Piper and Grudem's conclusion that, "Submission refers to a wife's divine calling to honor and affirm her husband's leadership and help carry it through according to her gifts," in *Recovering Biblical Manhood and Womanhood*, 61.

12. John Stott, *God's New Society* (Downers Grove, Ill.: InterVarsity Press, 1979), 219.

13. Hughes, *Ephesians*, 185.

14. Susan Foh in *Women and the Word of God* writes, "The Christian wife has the responsibility to grow in Christ, to know doctrine, to be able to speak the truth in love. . . . In addition, she is not to be silent when her husband sins (Matt. 18:15), but she is to teach and admonish him (Col. 3:16). However, she is to do all of these things with a submissive heart. . . . The Christian wife is neither passive nor mindless. She does not have to pretend that her husband is always right or hide her own talents or intelligence. She is to use her gifts for the upbuilding of the body of Christ, which includes her husband" (p. 186).

Chapter 5: *A Woman's Dignity*

1. Paul Settle, "One in Christ," *Equip for Ministry* 2, no. 4 (July–August 1996): 16.

2. See the manuscript data in *The Greek New Testament* of the United Bible Societies; and George W. Knight III, "Husbands and Wives as Analogues of Christ and the Church: Ephesians 5:21–33 and Colossians 3:18–19," in *Recovering Biblical Manhood and Womanhood*, 166.

3. Though Paul addresses "slaves" here (as Peter does in the parallel 1 Peter 2:18), we are wrong if we only interpret the words in the context of the despicable, chattel slavery of American history. The word translated "slave" in this passage most naturally refers to household servants, which included those in apprentice and indentured relationships as well as captured enemies and employed servants. Thus, Peter's instruction applies to all who by reason of training, occupation, or situation had their lives controlled by another. The spectrum of persons being addressed makes it appropriate for us to apply these words to modern employment situations.

4. The observation that the Bible never specifically tells husbands to submit to wives is an important caution for those who wish to say that the command to "submit to one another" removes all gender distinctions in the church. Far from removing respective authority/submission responsibilities in the home, the apostles are of one voice in the precise way they maintain the Bible's commitment to husband-headship and wife-submission while carefully contextualizing the expression of these roles in Christ's sacrificial use of authority and his noble example of submission. See note in Piper and Grudem, eds., *Recovering Biblical Manhood and Womanhood*, 493.

5. Note that in 1 Peter 3:7 the apostle commands husbands to treat their wives with *respect*, the same word he uses a few verses earlier (2:17) to describe how we should treat kings, among others.

6. David B. Calhoun, *Faith and Learning 1812–1868*, vol. 1 of *History of Princeton Seminary* (Edinburgh: Banner of Truth Trust, 1994), 173.

7. See the *Westminster Shorter Catechism*, question 6.

8. Ovey, "Equality but Not Symmetry," 1–4.

9. Susan Hunt in *The True Woman* offers this helpful commentary: "[E]very woman is not to submit to every man, but every married woman is to submit to her husband. The Scriptural command to women is . . . to 'be submissive to your husbands' (1 Peter 3:1). In Titus 2 we read that older women are to teach younger women to 'be subject to their husbands' . . . [T]he Biblical commands about women not usurping authority have reference to the home and church, not society in general" (p. 206).

10. Phoebe Hoban, "Women Who Run with the Trends," *Harper's Bazaar* (January 1994): 42.

11. A point articulately made by UCLA professor Patricia Marks Greenfield in "The Missing Half of Feminism," *St. Louis Post-Dispatch*, December 26, 1996, p. 7B.

12. John Angell James, *Female Piety* (1860; reprint, Pittsburgh: Soli Deo Gloria Publishers, 1994), 72.

Chapter 6: *A Woman's Desire*

1. Hunt, *The True Woman*, 103.

2. God speaks to Eve of her changed nature after sinning, saying, "Your desire will be for your husband" (Gen. 3:16). The words do not refer to her physical desire alone, for prior to her sin God had blessed both a man and wife with sexual attraction. Rather, the words refer to a woman's now corrupted desire for the man's very essence—control of his position, being, and heart, which (as the Genesis account of the fall has already made clear) is self-destructive to individuals and relationships. That the issue is actually control and not attraction is made clear by the words that follow ("Your desire will be for your husband, but he will rule over you." Compare the similar wording in Gen. 4:7). For a fuller discussion of these issues see Ray C. Ortlund Jr., "Male-Female Equality and Male Headship in Genesis 1–3," in *Recovering Biblical Manhood and Womanhood*, 108–9; Clowney, *The Church*, 219.

Part 3: *Sacrificial Partners*

1. Hunt, *The True Woman*, 30–32.

Chapter 7: *Each for the Other as Parents*

1. William Willimon, "Reaching and Teaching the Abandoned Generation," *Christian Century* 11, no. 29 (October 20, 1993): 1018.

2. Ibid.

3. David Blankenhorn, *Fatherless America* (New York: Basic Books, 1995), 2, 18–19. Blankenhorn cites: 57.7 percent of children in America were living with both parents in 1990—in 1960 the percentage was 80.6; the percentage of children living with a mother only was 7.7 percent in 1960—in 1990 the percentage rose to 21.6 percent; 36.3 percent of America's children were living apart from their biological fathers in 1990. By the year 2000 Blankenhorn says half of our children will grow up without fathers daily present.

4. Bonnidell Clouse, *Teaching for Moral Growth* (Wheaton: Victor, 1993), 67–68.

Chapter 8: *Each for the Other in Society*

1. The structure of the verse supports the classic Christian thought that biblical social transformation results from personal renewal and ecclesiastical practice moving outward to the structural reform of society as a whole (see David Jones, *Biblical Christian Ethics* [Grand Rapids: Baker, 1994], 155). In general, evangelical Christians have shown much concern for the former and little for the latter. The apostle Peter's development of Christian obligations in all these spheres demonstrates the spiritual connections they all share.

2. Churches vary on what they consider the biblical justifications for divorce. It seems to me that the clear biblical grounds for which God allows divorce are adultery (Matt.

5:31–32; 19:9; Rom. 7:2–3) and irremediable desertion (1 Cor. 7:15). Both terms, I believe, encapsulate the concept of unfaithfulness to the marriage covenant, which would include serious personal abuse and the endangerment of one's children. The issues are complex and it is not my intention to turn this note into a treatise on the biblical grounds for divorce. I want to be clear, however, that when the Bible *allows* certain grounds for divorce, it does not *require* persons who have such grounds to proceed toward termination of their marriages. On the contrary, Scripture enjoins all Christians as much as possible to act with prudence (seeking the counsel of their church) both in protecting their families and in promoting the testimony of God's unconditional love even to one who is guilty of wrong-doing (Rom. 12:17–21; 1 Peter 3:8–9; 4:8). God mercifully allows divorce where the marriage breach is so serious that continuance in the relationship is not tolerable, but God does not encourage divorce where forgiveness, counsel, and testimony may yet provide healing for the marriage or persons in it.

3. *Westminster Shorter Catechism*, question 27.

Bryan Chapell, Ph.D., is president of Covenant Theological Seminary. He and his wife, Kathy, have been married for more than twenty years. They are the parents of Colin, Jordan, Corinne, and Kaitlin. In addition to speaking widely in the United States and other countries, Bryan has written several books and pastored two churches. His communication and theology degrees are from Northwestern University, Covenant Theological Seminary, and Southern Illinois University.

To receive a copy of a small-group leader's guide for *Each for the Other,* contact the Media Office at Covenant Theological Seminary, 12330 Conway Road, St. Louis, MO 63141, 314-434-4044.